TOMORROW BEGINS NOW

TOMORROW BEGINS NOW

Teen Heroes Who Faced Down Injustice

Ava Lorelei Deakin

NEW DEGREE PRESS
COPYRIGHT © 2022 AVA LORELEI DEAKIN
All rights reserved.

TOMORROW BEGINS NOW
Teen Heroes Who Faced Down Injustice

ISBN
979-8-88504-537-7 *Paperback*
979-8-88504-863-7 *Kindle Ebook*
979-8-88504-653-4 *Digital Ebook*

*I dedicate this book to middle-school me. You
were so brave at a ridiculously young age.*

*To my mom and dad, who tirelessly supported
me throughout the lawsuit.*

*To my attorneys, who approached each
trial with kindness and humor.*

To Ms. Storm, who got me into history.

To the next kid who needs to be brave: I hope this book helps.

CONTENTS

Preface — 9

PART 1 — **ME + 1950s – 1980s** — **17**
Chapter 1 — Ava Deakin v. Ableism in Historic Districts (2019) — 19
Chapter 2 — Minnijean Brown Trickey v. Segregation (1957) — 45
Chapter 3 — Najah Najiy v. Racial Inequality (1963) — 63
Chapter 4 — Mary Beth Tinker v. Censorship (1969) — 77
Chapter 5 — Aaron Fricke v. Homophobia (1980) — 89
Chapter 6 — Bridgetta Bourne-Firl v. Ableism against Deaf People (1988) — 101

PART 2 — **2000s – 2010s** — **109**
Chapter 7 — Constance McMillen v. Homophobia (2010) — 111
Chapter 8 — Mary Kate Callahan v. Ableism in Sports (2012) — 123
Chapter 9 — Martín J. Batalla Vidal v. Unjust Deportation (2016) — 131

PART 3 — **2020s** — **141**
Chapter 10 — Gavin Grimm v. Transphobia (2021) — 143
Chapter 11 — Brandi Levy v. Digital Censorship (2021) — 153

Conclusion — 163
Acknowledgments — 165
Appendix — 169

PREFACE

I sat in my eighth-grade humanities class at the University of Chicago Laboratory Schools. I had just learned that morning of the Old Town Triangle lawsuit against me and my family and was feeling impossibly alone and unmotivated. Still, I was determined to focus—at least for this class period.

I cracked open the book we were reading for our civil rights unit: *Warriors Don't Cry*, an autobiography written by Little Rock Nine member Melba Pattillo-Beals. This was the first time I had read anything about a teen activist like myself. Reading her book inspired me to keep fighting in the legal system, and I sought out other stories of young people fighting for civil rights and liberties. I came across hundreds of cases from the early 1900s to the early 2020s, and each story made me feel less alone.

Many people believe only adults have impacted civil rights and liberties. This is not true. Adults and teenagers have fought side-by-side for civil rights and liberties throughout history, and both age groups have had great impacts on the world around them. Throughout US history, young people have organized protests and marches as a way of bringing people together and fighting for what they believe will make the world a better place.

Many people believe you must be exceptional to drive change. Western media is especially fond of this trope (McLaughlin, 2021). The concept of being the "Chosen One" is common in action movies, but in real life, exceptionality is not an innate trait. Most of the cases in this book began with young people being themselves. They began with young people going about their lives and recognizing a problem in what they saw around them. Exceptionality emerged from their reaction to the problem: fighting back. By fighting back and persevering, these young people grew to be exceptional.

Exceptionality is forged and honed.

How do I know these common beliefs are misconceptions? My name is Ava Lorelei Deakin, and I was a plaintiff in *Deakin v. Old Town Triangle Association*. I have a disability that requires me to wear leg braces and regularly use a wheelchair. I was thirteen when I started my fight for disability rights under the Fair Housing Act. By the end, I was sixteen and finally able to make accessible modifications to my house as well as co-chair a committee who ensured accessibility and inclusion within my Chicago community.

This book offers readers a glimpse into the journeys of modern civil rights activists in their own words. I hope reading this book will encourage young people to engage in activism, in small and big ways. Whether it's organizing/attending a local protest or fighting in court, we can all make a difference. I also hope these stories of shared fortitude will help quell the feelings of loneliness that are often experienced while fighting for a cause.

In this book, I highlight the cases that inspired *me* to keep fighting while being the lead plaintiff in a federal discrimination lawsuit. These cases took place across decades, from 1957 to 2021, with a total of eleven activists featured. Before I start, I will clarify some terminology used in this book.

Definitions of Terms

Throughout this book, you will see many cases of young people filing lawsuits at various judiciary levels.

- A *protected class* is a group of people who are eligible for special legal protection from discrimination (Cornell Law School, 2022). Protected class designation seeks to protect people against discrimination based on characteristics. The protected classes discussed in this book are:
- race
- gender
- sexuality
- disability

(Dover, 2020)

Deferred Action for Childhood Arrivals (DACA) recipients are also included in this book, but they are considered to have protected *status* instead of being a *protected class*.

- A *lawsuit* is a claim or dispute that is brought to court for a ruling (Cornell Law School, 2022).

- *Representation* is the attorney or law firm who argues for a person in court (Cornell Law School, 2022).

  - An example of representation is the American Civil Liberties Union, the organization who represented Brandi Levy in *Levy v. Mahanoy Area School District*.

- A *protest* is the public's way of expressing disapproval through marches, proposed bills, and more (Cornell Law School, 2022).

- A *plaintiff* is the person who starts a lawsuit (Cornell Law School, 2022).

- *Appealing* a case means one of the parties in the lawsuit is unhappy with the ruling and wants another court to take a look at it. Appealing a case most often leads to the case going to a higher court (Cornell Law School, 2022).

There are three levels of courts in the United States (from highest to lowest):

- The *Supreme Court* is the highest level of court in the United States. This court has the *final* say if a lawsuit reaches that level (United States Department of Justice, 2022). As a result, many of the cases appealed to the Supreme Court are looked to as *precedent*. A *precedent* is a case (or event) that previously happened and is looked to as an example or guide of how future cases should be handled. In terms of the Supreme Court, a *precedent* is legally binding unless it is overturned.

- An excellent example of a *precedent*-setting case is *Tinker v. Des Moines*. Mary Beth Tinker's case for students' Freedom of Speech was appealed to the Supreme Court and is still used as a reference in cases—over fifty years later (ACLU, 2022).

- *Federal courts* hear cases that involve the constitutionality of laws, discrimination lawsuits, or lawsuits between states (United States Department of Justice, 2022).

  - An example of this is my own case, *Deakin v. OTTA*, where I fought for disability rights. As it was a discrimination lawsuit, it was considered a *federal* lawsuit.

- *The court of appeals* consist of twelve *circuit courts* (courts in between states that are connected by "circuits") that preside over specific geographic regions in the United States (e.g., Ohio is in the sixth circuit, which also oversees Kentucky, Minnesota, and Tennessee). *Appellate courts* determine, if the case is *appealed*, whether existing laws have been properly applied in lower court rulings (United States Courts, 2022).

  - Before Gavin Grimm's case (*Grimm v. Gloucester County Independent School District*) was appealed to the Supreme Court, his case went through the appellate courts. Though he won in the initial lawsuit, his school appealed the decision to an appellate court, where the judge ruled against Gavin. The decisions of the presiding judges were appealed until they surpassed the appellate courts and made it to the Supreme Court via representation by the American Civil Liberties Union (ACLU).

I believe we can live in a just world if we challenge the status quo. Civil rights and liberties can only be attained and strengthened if we question the way things are done and consider what course of action would make the world a more welcoming place for everyone. Young people have always helped in pushing society forward—though there is a surprising lack of teen perspective when talking about civil rights. The history of the fight for civil rights and liberties has largely been told through textbooks with few details about the *people* involved in these cases.

Whether you're interested in activism, learning more about civil rights and liberties, or are already fighting for civil rights and liberties, I hope this book provides at least one story in which you can see a little bit of your own experience.

The world can be an amazing place. Through finding resources, gaining alliances, honing exceptionality, and understanding the legal system, I believe we can make the world better—one case at a time.

PART 1

ME + 1950s - 1980s

CHAPTER 1
2019

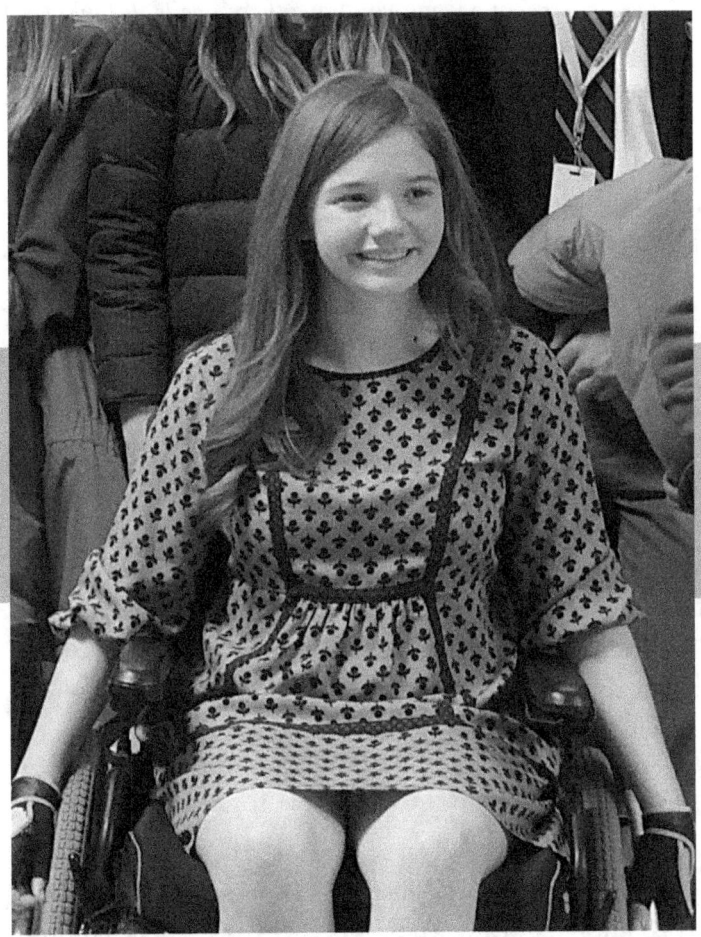

Available from: Ava Deakin

AVA LORELEI DEAKIN VS. ABLEISM IN HISTORIC DISTRICTS

> *I understand that the people who purchased the house have a child that requires special needs. What I don't understand is why they chose to buy a house in a Landmark Zone when you have these needs. I don't mean to be heartless or uncaring, but this is not the neighborhood for that.* —Old Town Triangle Association President

My heart dropped. He meant *me*. I was "that." This was all my fault.

The year was 2017. It had been nearly two years since my family had begun the process of acquiring the necessary permits for the accessible renovations to a dilapidated 1880s building in the Old Town Triangle, a "Landmarked" neighborhood of 524 historic homes in Chicago. We came to learn that our new house at 1848 North Lincoln was widely known in the neighborhood as the "Rat House." It reeked of cigarettes and animal urine and was in bad condition from top to bottom. The place hadn't been loved in decades. Despite its dilapidated state, Mom committed to saving it and making it fully accessible for me—as well as making it a home for our growing family.

I have been dealing with an undiagnosed neurological condition that affected my legs since I was two years old. Because of my condition, I wear leg braces (a.k.a. Ankle-Foot Orthosis/ AFOs) every day and use a wheelchair for long distances.

During my seventh-grade year, I had surgery on both my legs and feet. I spent most of the school year recovering at the Shirley Ryan Ability Lab and attending classes through Skype.

It was a challenging way to learn, and staying connected to my classmates and teachers was difficult. My eighth-grade year was supposed to be the year I could finally go back to school, make more friends, and just be a kid.

But that didn't happen.

Plans for our house were exciting: a new bedroom, a barrier-free entrance inside the garage that replaced the old coal house, and an elevator about the size of a closet that would provide access to every level of the house. Anywhere I wanted to go, my wheelchair could take me. Despite the time it took to get started, all was well with the house for about seven months.

The neighborhood itself was quaint. The bells of St. Michael's tolled over the Old Town Triangle. The houses, frozen in time, sat compactly in the shadow of the 170-year-old church. Every corner the Chicago sun touched had the mark of the twenty-first century, including curb cuts, paved streets, and metal skyscrapers, but where the sun wasn't watching, nothing had changed. The Old Town Triangle's row-houses creaked with chipped gingerbread trim that had remained affixed to the edges of Victorian roofs.

The Old Town Triangle Association (OTTA), a committee of neighborhood residents who had controlled area development since the late 1940s, did not like the transformation at 1848 North Lincoln. In the summer of 2018, the city alderman for our area—the forty-third ward—and the OTTA historic committee demanded an explanation. This was despite two years of work with the city to obtain the permits that included approvals from the State of Illinois and City of Chicago Landmarks Departments.

The project was up for review. The city suddenly issued a "Stop Work" order, stating there was some sort of administrative zoning error while approving the original permits. Many people were confused because it had taken forever to get things going and now we were stopping. *Why?*

The school bus carried me home, just as it had every other day of the eighth grade. It had turned cold in Chicago and the wind was smashing waves against the Lake Michigan seawall along Lake Shore Drive. I leaned my forehead against the cool window and watched Buckingham Fountain, the skyscrapers in the Loop, the Ferris wheel at Navy Pier, and the zoo slide by as we made our way to the northside.

My mom was waiting for me at the bus stop, bundled up in a full-length puffer coat that I jokingly called the "Michelin Man." Mom gave me her arm to steady me as I awkwardly stepped off the bus, and the driver handed down my wheeled backpack and glittery pink cross-body lunchbox.

"We need to talk about something important," Mom said quietly as we slowly walked arm in arm to the street corner. I looked up at her, surprised. "It's about the new house and the new neighbors."

As I would come to understand later, this was not my last bus ride of middle school, but the last of my childhood.

We stepped inside our condo and made our way over to the couch. "Ava," Mom said, "Dad got a call from a reporter who is writing a story about us—about the modifications we are making to the back of the new house to make it accessible for you. Apparently, someone who is not a fan of our project reached out to this news site, 'Block Club,' encouraging them to investigate. Some Old Town Triangle neighbors have already been interviewed. The reporter said he has some public letters from Old Town Triangle Association members that he would be referencing. We need to decide if we want to provide comments for the article or pass on it."

"How bad are the letters?"

With some hesitation, my mother replied, "Bad." She picked up a pile of papers and held them out so I could read them. "About two weeks ago, our zoning attorney, Nick, sent these to me. They're letters of opposition for the accessible modifications we are making. These letters were sent to everyone from our alderman to the mayor and lots of others. They contain some pretty hurtful language…" She sighed. "I didn't want you to see these, but if they are going to be published, you need to decide for yourself what you think about them."

My temples started to hurt. Mom swallowed hard and began: "The first letter is from the OTTA president. I've never met him, but I heard he has a daughter about the same age as you." I nodded solemnly. Mom continued, "He wrote,

'I understand that the people who purchased the house have a child that requires special needs. What I don't understand is why they chose to buy a house in a Landmark Zone when you

have these needs. I don't mean to be heartless or uncaring but this is not the neighborhood for that."

He further claimed my *needs* could be better met in other neighborhoods, and my parents should have *"put their child's needs first and moved to a neighborhood more conducive to her needs [...] Here you conform to the rules, not the other way around."*

The letter went on for two pages, not only threatening us, but threatening the Landmarks people and the alderman with legal action. He concluded that if it didn't go his way, he would build his own garage on his two properties.

We read through the stack of letters, each one making me feel increasingly sick. We had about a dozen different neighbors with the same painful message: I didn't fit, and they wanted to keep it that way.

I was baffled and hurt. "Mom, what rules do they think we've broken? I know you worked with the Buildings Department, City Landmarks, Illinois Historic Preservation Office, and the Art Institute of Chicago—and followed the guidelines from the National Park Service on how to make historic properties accessible. What did we miss?"

"Ava, I don't think it is written rules they are talking about… we followed the letter of the law. I think this is really about the power OTTA has derived through unwritten rules for the past seventy years. I know the names and faces have changed over time, but the power and control they exert over the neighborhood has remained the same. They don't want anything to change, even if it's allowed by the Landmarks Department, who actually has the final authority…"

I realized the issue was much bigger than me. I agreed to be a part of the Block Club article, which was just the beginning.

***

The Fair Housing Act (FHA) was signed into law in 1968. It declared that discrimination against people buying or renting a house was prohibited. Despite this legislation, along with the Americans with Disabilities Act of 1990, there is still a housing deficiency for people with disabilities (Access Living of Metropolitan Chicago, 2018).

Discrimination against people with disabilities is pervasive. For the past several years, the largest percentage of complaints filed with the US Department of Housing and Urban Development concerned allegations of disability-based discrimination. In 2015, the percentage of complaints was 55.8 percent. In 2016, the percentage rose to 58.5 percent. Finally, in 2017, complaints concerning allegations of disability-based discrimination made up 59.4 percent of all the complaints—a 106 percent increase from 2015 (Access Living of Metropolitan Chicago, 2018).

***

The alderman informed my parents they had to meet with the OTTA and review the project. My parents had prepared a short summary detailing the renovation plans.

The next morning, Mom told me about the comments made during the meeting. One neighbor on the Historic Planning committee compared me to a "luxury car" and said, like a luxury car in this neighborhood of tiny garages, I "didn't fit." She told my parents it would be best to leave the neighborhood, and we could find many other neighborhoods that were more conducive to my needs. Another neighbor asked several times, "Why would a family with your needs buy a home in our neighborhood?" and they were determined to find out.

***

Click! An older man stood near me with his phone raised, and it looked like he was recording. I had noticed him on the corner down the street from my school bus stop and had assumed he was walking elsewhere, but he was following me to my house. His dog tugged on its leash as I scurried up the stairs to my front door. I slammed the door shut and fumbled with the lock. My head spun. *What just happened? Who is he? What is he going to do with those pictures?* I ran to my mother.

"Mom, Mom!" I said, breathless as I made my way over to the couch. "There was a guy outside taking pictures of me! I think he was taking pictures of my legs. He followed me across the street, and he's standing at the bottom of the stairs—"

My mother looked at me, shocked. "*He's standing at the bottom of the stairs?*" She dashed outside, not even stopping to put her shoes on, but he was gone. "Ava," she asked, "who was it? Did you get a good look at him?"

My answers were "Yes" and "No." I had seen him, but I had no idea who he might be.

After my encounter with the stalker, I wasn't allowed to leave the house or get on the bus by myself. Either the school bus driver, my babysitter, or my mom would wait for the bus with me or watch to make sure I got into my house safely. I felt suffocated by the constant surveillance, but I was too scared to go anywhere without it. Making friends proved difficult without the ability to go out after school.

Another meeting with the OTTA was scheduled by the alderman's office. My parents and I discussed whether I should attend. Eventually, it was decided that things were too unpredictable, and it was better for me to stay home.

The meeting turned out to be more of an ambush on the OTTA's part. They were offended by my family's efforts to move forward with the renovations and signaled their intentions to oppose us more broadly.

The Association blamed my parents, and by extension, me. My mom and dad were "bad parents" for trying to put me in a neighborhood where I "didn't fit in" and for trying to get "special treatment" in terms of adding accessibility features, as if they were luxury, nonessential additions to our house. Most shockingly, Mom overheard members of the OTTA talking in front of her while they crowded around a phone. They were watching the stalker's video of me walking up the stairs. *"I saw the ramp. I saw her walking up the stairs. She was definitely walking. She has what she needs, see? She doesn't even have a wheelchair accessible parking space. They have a ramp."* They were the ones who had followed me home.

The OTTA members further suggested we stay in our present condo, totally missing the point that the excessive stairs were the reason we were moving in the first place. They even suggested we build some sort of hidden, underground garage—a "Batcave" of sorts—under our new house, where my "unsightly handicap access" could be buried: an impossible proposition because building under the house's foundation in that way would have made the entire house susceptible to caving in at any moment.

One thing was crystal clear: the accessible modifications for our home, previously approved by the Landmarks Department, were not good enough for the OTTA, and accommodating a kid with a disability was more than the neighborhood could withstand.

The OTTA board decided to leverage the neighborhood's plentiful assets to discourage me and my family from continuing with our plans. The OTTA regularly hosted a popular and successful annual art fair that added to the neighborhood bank account, which was primarily used for charity. We found out later they used some of the cash to hire attorneys and public relations firms, and created email campaigns, online polls, and social media posts against us.

OTTA.com posted all the legal filings and committee meeting notes; the neighborhood newsletter also publicized events, and the email mailing list was more than six hundred names long. All this combined with social media posts led to more serious actions taken by more and more people.

My father received phone calls and text messages threatening our family, some of them included "Hopefully you are changing your plans or selling the project. Lots of people are mad...Alderman is going to block. Burning time and money as is... Not a good entry to the community" and "If you don't do what I ask, you will replace another neighbor as the most hated person in the neighborhood."

Our construction crews were verbally assaulted, the construction site was vandalized, and tossing dog waste all over the property became a new sport. Lots of notes and press releases were posted by the Triangle's committee stating how hard they had tried to work with us. We received calls from the alderman's office about the latest emails and pictures sent from someone in the Old Town Triangle. Scores of accusations (including that we were "puppet masters" who had set out to ruin the Old Town Triangle) circulated in-person and online. They said our attorney was corrupt, that we were "fixing" city committees, that I didn't really need the accommodations and, even if I *did* need them, I would soon be off to college.

As hard as my parents tried, they couldn't protect me from the case because it was too pervasive. My peers and teachers saw the articles. My friends from *elementary school* saw the articles. My physical therapists, past and present, saw the articles. I couldn't escape. At thirteen, it was difficult to sort through all the drama. It felt like David versus Goliath.

Since the first article, the Block Club had published more posts about us, and all the articles were overwhelmingly positive (Ballew, 2018). People saw what OTTA stood for and blasted them. Hundreds of comments poured in, spilling over to Reddit as well and onto the pages of NextDoor.com. The Facebook pages for OTTA were swamped with angry comments. For the first time since the case began, I stopped blaming myself.

***

Ava and her supporters waiting in the lobby of City Hall for the ZBA hearing to start. (Image provided by Andrew Diehlmann)

As we waited in the second-floor lobby of City Hall in downtown Chicago for the Zoning Board of Appeals (ZBA) hearing, which was delayed four months by the OTTA, my classmates, friends, and family began gathering for what would turn out to be a *really* long day. I was nervous, but the overwhelming support was just what I needed. Glittery homemade signs of support, along with lots of anxious laughter, filled the space. I avoided the crowd for the most part. I was nervous and trembling. I was in awe of the number of people who had come to support me. I had expected four or five people outside of my family to attend—around twenty had already shown up. The volume of people amassing in the lobby also gave me a twinge of stage fright. I had been in theater productions at school, but in a play, there is a *script*, and you know what you're *supposed* to say. City Hall was *improv*, which was not my strong suit. To calm myself, I mentally reviewed a thirty-page Google Doc of bullet points on disability history I had created. I had studied the document every day leading up to the hearing, assuring myself that, if I committed it exactly to memory, I would be ready.

Mom and I passed out handmade, multicolored ribbons for every supporter to wear. They thanked us and asked questions about the case, which I answered heartily but quickly. Everyone reassured me that we would win. I was feeling confident too, even though this was new to all of us.

Twenty cases were heard before ours. Apparently the ZBA knew ours was going to be a lengthy hearing and decided to handle it last to allow enough time for both sides to present. Five hours later, case number twenty-one was called.

Ava Deakin waiting to testify while her supporters stand in the back. (Image provided by Lisa Diehlmann)

More than thirty people stood in support of us as the hearing began. The board chair took time to recognize them. The OTTA members were frustrated, and they complained the children in attendance would play on the sympathies of the ZBA. The ZBA assuaged the OTTA's concerns and told the children to sit.

Ava's supporters holding up signs before being asked to sit down. (Image provided by Lisa Diehlmann)

Most of the hearing was on the zoning law and what certain codes meant—and how all that applied. I testified about my own needs and presented a survey of homes in the Old Town Triangle with street-facing garages, which turned out to total more than fifty. Basically, OTTA said what we were proposing was so out of character that it would ruin the property values of the whole neighborhood. Yet, there were more than fifty similar homes.

The Mayor's Office for People with Disabilities and The Chicago Commission on Human Relations had sent letters of support. Mr. Stolar, a longtime homeowner who lived just down the street from our house, also testified in support. The wife and daughter of Dr. Henry Betts, an advocate for people with disabilities who had helped pass the Americans with Disabilities Act (ADA), sent support. The Betts family had been Triangle residents for decades. I felt the weight gradually lifting from my young shoulders.

The OTTA had one last move. We had learned a couple of weeks before the ZBA hearing that they had hired an "Accessibility Architect" to testify against our plans. She told the ZBA that our plans were not safe for me, and the home was not accessible. What she proposed was digging down underneath our house with a long driveway that would run the length of the yard as the solution. She cited some regulations and some rather simple assumptions. After a few minutes of questioning, her arguments fell apart. Our architect, John DeSalvo, pointed out the city had approved the plans and testified that all was within code and safe.

Access Living's Mary Rosenberg spoke clearly about the law and the challenge people with disabilities have in finding accessible housing.

> *Less than 1 percent of the nation's housing stock is accessible to those with moderate physical disabilities and less than 1 percent is accessible to those who use wheelchairs. [...] Where there is tension between historical landmark preservation and accessibility, accessibility is paramount. The obligation to make buildings accessible to people with disabilities is not eliminated because the building or neighborhood is historic under either the Fair Housing Act or the Americans with Disabilities Act.* —Mary Rosenberg

Mary went on to cite and disprove the three most common discriminatory beliefs regarding people with disabilities, which were being promoted by the Old Town Triangle Association:

- "*...if the family is allowed to build this garage, other neighbors will be emboldened to renovate their properties any way they see fit. This is patently untrue. Other people would have the same right to renovations only if they had a similar disability-related need.*"

- "*...the garage interferes with the historical value of the neighborhood or that because the family has a daughter with a disability it should not have moved to this historic area. The Fair Housing Act prohibits these types of beliefs and speculation as an "exclusion of* individuals based upon fear, speculation, or stereotype about a particular disability or persons with disabilities in general."

- "...to insist people with disabilities not move into a particular neighborhood because the housing would need to be modified to fit their needs is simple NIMBYism. It is the same as an outright prohibition against people with disabilities living in the neighborhood."

The hearing ended with a neighbor shouting "She should stay where she is!" and two others from OTTA wishing me and my mom "Merry Christmas" through gritted teeth, saying, "It looks like we are going to be neighbors!"

I went with a few of my peers to a Starbucks while we waited for their parents to pick them up. When everyone was safe with their families, I sat with my aunt and uncle, awaiting my mom's arrival. She had stayed behind in the courtroom to hear the decision. Just after my uncle surprised me with a ginormous hot chocolate, my mom came in grinning from ear to ear.

The ZBA had ruled in our favor, 5-0.

Left to right: Bill Deakin, Ava Lorelei Deakin, Lisa Diehlmann, and Ava's aunt and uncle in the Starbucks where they heard the court victory. (Image provided by Lisa Diehlmann)

I was relieved with the results. My friends, family, and advocates for people with disabilities were enthusiastic in their support. I met a lot of new people—people like me—who faced challenges that were hard to understand.

We also began to see notes of support from a few people in the Triangle who were put off by OTTA. It all felt good, but in truth, I was ready to move on, finish the eighth grade, and get ready for high school!

By late March, all had been quiet, and school was the normal routine. Mom and Dad received word that OTTA and those people who had wished us a "Merry Christmas" were going to appeal the 5-0 Zoning decision and sue us and the Chicago Zoning Board of Appeals. They also defamed our attorney for alleged illegal lobbying. This halted construction on our home once again.

Dad was told by several people that the OTTA was going to bankrupt us by keeping the case going in the courts. One of the Old Town Triangle residents in a house not far from ours had endured thirteen years of OTTA legal actions.

After the new lawsuit dragged on for eight months, I decided I had to do something: I decided I had to study! In Illinois, you study the US Constitution in the eighth grade and that was coming in handy. I further educated myself on disability history and modern disability law, dissecting how historical events had led to the rights and protections today, including within historic zones. I *had* to make some sense out of the situation.

Michael Allen, a Washington DC attorney who had litigated many cases for people with disabilities, made a trip to see us. He had been talking with my parents and wanted to talk with me too.

"Ava, you have done nothing wrong. The adults are acting badly," he explained. "People with disabilities have the right, a protected civil right, to live anywhere—including in historic districts. Don't listen to the OTTA."

That day, I decided to file a discrimination lawsuit. I knew I had to stand up for myself and take control of my future—at least where and how I was going to live.

My case was no longer about zoning: It was about civil rights. My attorneys, Michael Allen and Tahir Duckett, committed to working closely with me. Filing a civil rights lawsuit in federal court was difficult, but I had to stand up for myself.

On December 17, 2019, Case 1:19-Cv-08229 was filed: **In THE UNITED STATES DISTRICT COURT FOR THE NORTHERN DISTRICT OF ILLINOIS Eastern Division.**

AVA DEAKIN, by her parents and next friends, WILLIAM J. DEAKIN and LISA M. DIEHLMANN, et al.,

Plaintiffs, v. Case No. 19-8229

OLD TOWN TRIANGLE ASSOCIATION, *Defendant.*

There was a lot to digest in those twenty-five pages. I had read extensively about the Americans with Disabilities Act (ADA) that year and learned a lot from Attorney Mary Rosenberg at *Access Living*. Now, I was going to live it. The first lesson was on the Federal Fair Housing Act of 1988.

Our court filing described it this way:

The OTTA's actions described herein amount to disability discrimination in violation of the FHA and its implementing regulations at 24 C.F.R. Part 100. In passing the FHA's 1988 amendments, which added robust protection for people with disabilities, Congress clearly pronounced "a national commitment to end the unnecessary exclusion of persons with [disabilities] from the American mainstream." H.R. Rep. No. 711, 100th Cong., 2d Sess. 18 (1988), reprinted at 1988 U.S. Code Cong. & Admin. News 2173, 2179. Precisely such exclusion is at issue here.

Lack of accessible housing is one of the key barriers to the independence, integration, and full citizenship for people with disabilities. That the OTTA's vitriolic discrimination on the basis of disability lies beneath the thinnest veneer of concern for historic preservation is nothing new—community resistance to people with disabilities is often shrouded in pretextual "quality of neighborhood" concerns that are designed to exclude. Nonetheless, the FHA prohibits that resistance where, as here, it is designed to make housing unavailable because of a person's disability; becomes harassing, coercive, and intimidating; indicates a preference with respect to the sale of a dwelling based on disability; or otherwise interferes with the enjoyment of rights guaranteed by federal law.

With the filing, public discussion became more intense. Things began to change. We began to hear from neighbors—most of whom we had never met—who were angry and embarrassed by the OTTA's position. These neighbors started to become proactive.

The annual election of the OTTA board was a defining step. Old Town Triangle residents campaigned to replace the board members who had been leading the opposition to our project.

> *URGENT! OTTA Election January '21 - Important Considerations. With all due respect to the work and dedication of the current board, it is time for a change. As active OTTA members and former officers, we want to share with you our concerns that call into question the leadership of the current Board and should be more widely known before votes are cast in the upcoming election on January 28th.* —Shelly Murphy, Sasha Mayoras, Vi Daley, Philip Graff (Murphy et al, 2021)

Over the previous two years, there had been thousands of social media posts, dozens of articles in the media, and television and radio coverage that had been largely powerful and supportive. Yet it was the passionate writing of these four OTT residents that changed the opinions of the majority of our future neighbors. In January 2021, most of the board was voted out. The neighborhood that for two years had been plastered with "Hate Has No Home Here" posters was finally living up to the motto.

The COVID-19 pandemic seemed to add a few weeks to every step along the way. I distinctly remember refreshing the page in quarantine to see when our next trial date would be. *Reload. Reload.* The trial dates in the US Court of Appeals for the Seventh District seemed to always be six months out. We finally nailed down a date in March 2021—about two and a half years after hearing from the OTTA and the alderman for the first time. US Magistrate Judge M. David Weisman took charge of the hearing.

It was a weird day. Rather than being in court, we were on Zoom. The setup was three separate breakout rooms: one for us, one for OTTA, and one for the judge. Opening remarks by the judge established the rules, and we took our turns arguing our cases. Our lawyers were perfect. Their explanations and arguments were succinct and persuasive and gave me confidence that we would reach a favorable outcome.

Several hours later, we settled the lawsuit. For the first time since the problems began, I finally felt like I could take a moment to breathe. *We did it!*

A few weeks later, we released the following statement:

> The Deakin family and the Old Town Triangle Association (OTTA) are pleased to announce that they have amicably resolved any dispute between them concerning renovations to 1848 North Lincoln Avenue. OTTA looks forward to welcoming the Deakins to the Triangle in the summer of 2021.

> The Deakins and OTTA have agreed to continue working together in the coming years by forming an Accessibility Committee to ensure that the Old Town Triangle Historic District and the iconic OTTA Art Fair are made even more accessible to—and welcoming for—people with disabilities. They also welcome Access Living as a participant in the Art Fair starting in 2021. The remainder of the settlement terms are confidential (Old Town Triangle Association, 2022).

Throughout the case, I had made an active effort to seek out other stories of teen activists. By the end, I was feeling much more connected and confident. Having to stand up for myself and go to the podium encouraged me and gave me some practice talking about myself in general. I saw how things could change if I used my voice. Once I saw I was actually helping other people and my story was being used as a case study in the Columbia Law Review and college lectures, I not only realized I could effect change but was also reassured I had been doing the right thing (Harris, 2019).

Ava Lorelei Deakin (Image provided by Lisa Diehlmann)

Now, I'm still fighting for accessibility. I became the honorary co-chair of the Old Town Triangle's Accessibility Committee, and I established my school's first ever Accessibility Committee. I watch PIXAR movies in my free time and draw whenever I have a chance. Right now, I'm looking at colleges and figuring out what I want in life. The only thing I know is that this is what it's all about—fighting for our rights and making the world a better place for everyone.

CHAPTER 2
1957

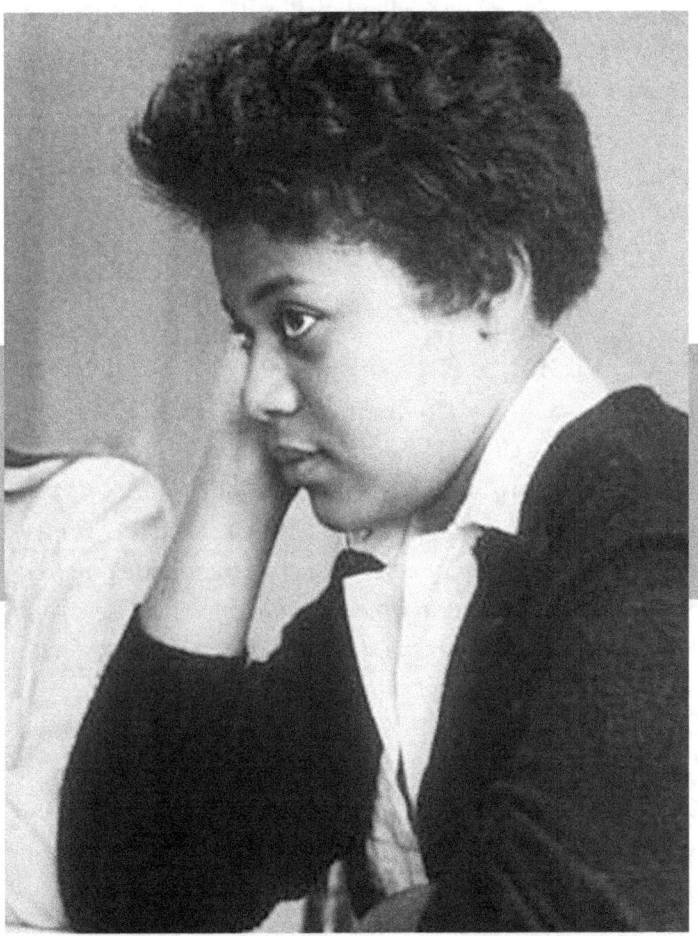

Gertrude Samuels/Archive Photos via Getty Images

MINNIJEAN BROWN TRICKEY VS. SEGREGATION

When I was going through the legal system, the first case to get my attention was the case of the Little Rock Nine. I remember sitting in my eighth-grade humanities class and annotating *Warriors Don't Cry* by Melba Pattillo-Beals. The story was about the Little Rock Nine's struggle with segregation in the Jim Crow South and how they fought for racial equality.

Shortly after reading *Warriors Don't Cry*, I wrote the following email to Melba on March 16, 2019:

Dear Ms. Patillo-Beals,

My name is Ava Lorelei Deakin, and I am writing to you to thank you. In my Humanities class, we read your book "Warriors Don't Cry". At the time, I was facing ability-based segregation from a neighbourhood that didn't want any people with disabilities to move in. This was an issue, since I use a wheelchair (I named it Winston) frequently due to a degenerative neurological condition that affects my legs. Your book helped me navigate the situation, and provided me with comfort that things could get better.

I had to testify in court on December 22nd, to the Zoning Board Association after four continuances. We won the case 5 - 0. Now we are waiting for the neighbours to sue us personally, or to sue the city. It's almost guaranteed.

Thank you again for writing your book. I truly appreciate it.

Best, A. L. Deakin

I was ecstatic when I got a response a week later.

Another part of *Warriors Don't Cry* I probably remember most, was that of Minnijean Brown spilling chili on a racist classmate. The story stuck with me throughout my lawsuit as a demonstration of strength, and it is one of the few parts of *Warriors Don't Cry* that I can vividly recall reading.

Even after my class was finished with the civil rights unit, I looked further into the Little Rock Nine's case and discovered an online lecture by Minnijean at the National Park College. This was toward the end of my own case, and I remember feeling overcome by her speech. I am honored to present Minnijean's story in her own words.

***

[Life before attending Central High School was] just peaceful as anything. [...] it was a segregated society, things were segregated in that [...] we couldn't go to movie theaters downtown. We sat in the balcony, there were periods of "colored" and "white" water fountains [...] but our community, our families managed to create parallel things. [...] If you didn't want to sit on the back of the bus, you just walked where you were going. And there were all these ways of just thinking, "let them be them, we'll be us." [...] We'll have activities, we'll have church, which was, for me, more of a social activity.

In 1957, in Little Rock, Arkansas, Minnijean and eight other Black students were selected to attend the all-white high school, Central High, for the purpose of racial integration. This group became known as the Little Rock Nine.

Before attending Central High School, Minnijean had been enrolled at Horace Mann High School. During her time at Horace Mann, she became aware that she was not receiving the same quality of education as Central High students. The news that she had been chosen to go to one of Little Rock's all-white high schools came as a shock. She had signed up for it, but she never expected to be chosen. She had seen Central before—she passed it every day on the way to Horace Mann.

Well, the truth is I decided to go to Central 'cause it was there and it was considered the most beautiful high school in America and it was within walking distance of my house. And so, when the announcement came, "if you're interested to go into Central," I just put my name on the list.

Minnijean stepped out of the car and looked up at the towering main building of Central High School. She caught her breath. Slowly, she began to move through the crowd. A sea of white faces glared at her, sizing her up. Eyes darted from her head to her shoes to her friends, each little fold on her dress giving rise to harsh whispers. Jeers sounded as Minnijean and her eight companions—Melba Beals, Ernest Green, Elizabeth Eckford, Jefferson Thomas, Terrence Roberts, Carlotta Walls, Gloria Ray, and Thelma Mothershed—made their way up the steps. She allowed herself a slight sigh of relief. *At least I won't be alone.*

She turned and looked at the crowd following her up the steps. Most seemed curious about the new students as brows furrowed over small, confused smiles. Minnijean caught a glimpse of some students whose eyes were already teeming with malice. She froze mid-step, her ribcage hollow. A bracing grimace inched onto her face.

Two of the girls were my best friends, Melba Pattillo and Thelma Mothershed, and we were thinking we would walk together to Central, where we were stupid enough, just to think we could walk there.

A hand touched her shoulder. "Minnijean," said Melba. Minnijean didn't look over.

"Minnijean!"

Minnijean looked at her quizzically.

"We have to go inside."

She nodded and followed her friends inside.

Uneasiness fell over Minnijean as she walked out of the sweltering heat and into the tiled halls. The floor clicked underneath her polished Mary Janes as she took it all in. (Millard Fillmore's Bathtub, 2022).

Well, Minnijean, she thought, *this is it. You can do this. For them.* Images of her three younger siblings flooded her mind. She took a deep breath, stabilized her trembling hands, and marched to her first class...

...there were all these people who were absolutely mindless, which is how I see violence— when people are completely non thinking, no intellect, no thought,

MINNIJEAN BROWN TRICKEY V. SEGREGATION (1957)

just being mindless with hatred. It was really shocking because I hadn't ever been hated in my life. I was scared to death [...] you can't see the shaking in the still pictures, but I was shaking my whole body. And I said to myself, "Well, you can act like this, but I'll be back." And I wasn't even sure how I would get back. But I was saying to myself, you're not going to stop me with your behavior, with your hate. And we do, we make those decisions, when we're fourteen or twelve or fifteen, because we see things and we just make decisions. So, that's how it was. I saw them as mindless and I thought, "I'll never be like that. I will never be led, nor will I choose to behave like that."

***

The room went silent. Minnijean's face went slack, realizing what had happened. Her fists released and her hands flew to her biceps, as if creating a shield around herself. The boy glared at her, his eyes flaming from under a thick layer of tomato soup. The soup trickled down his arms, oozing through and staining his white, button-up shirt. He pushed up his sleeves and stomped over, putting his soup-drenched face close to hers. Their noses were barely an inch apart. Minnijean's lungs felt like chasms, trapping her breath deep in her stomach. She took a delayed step back, bumping into the person ahead of her in line. She swiveled her head around and was met with an ocean of glaring eyes.

It was scary [...] There were two lunch periods and so at least there were a thousand kids in that lunch

[...] *I think it's perfectly an example of the school who would not see that it was [...] They were slamming against me. Students might have knocked it out of my hand, I might have.*

***

Minnijean toed into her vice principal's office. The vice principal looked up from her glasses and sighed. She inhaled, her shoulders rising, as she tried to manage a sentence. "Minnijean…what…"—the vice principal propped herself up begrudgingly, hastily fixing a stray hair from her tight bun—"What did you do?"

"Well, Miss…"

Minnijean explained everything to her vice principal, each word garnering an exponentially horrified and disgusted expression, until her advisor had seemed to have melted into the desk.

"Did you do it on purpose?" her exasperated advisor asked.

Minnijean remained stoic—she was used to this spiel.

"*Accidentally* on purpose."

> *When I went to the girl vice principal, she said, "Oh, Minnijean, what did you…" Her usual spiel. "Did you do it on purpose?" And I said, "Accidentally on purpose." Because you have to always be resisting their craziness. And I can't tell you whether it was accidental or on purpose because it happened so fast, but that was my way up.*

After being suspended, Minnijean came back to school to face an even more violent and intense backlash. She was constantly verbally and physically assaulted, and students began targeting her more overtly, regardless of whether adults were present or not.

The National Guard—a state-based military force primarily used to address issues within the *state* security rather than *national* security—was eventually instated in the halls of Central High to protect the Little Rock Nine from the harassment of their peers, but their presence did little to help. In fact, their presence just taught the mob to be faster and *sneakier*.

> *Even though there were Arkansas National Guard in the hallway at a certain point, they saw what they wanted to see, because they were Southern boys and things happened just quickly [...] Somebody could spit on you. [...] Somebody could spray ink, some bruiser would slam you against the wall and everything was done with a great deal of speed and intensity. [...] So it was always scary, but you didn't know what was going to happen. Assemblies were really bad because everybody went into the assembly in a rush. And so, our legs were always bruised after assemblies because some of the boys wore what they call heel plates, heel and toe plates like cat shoes.*

Every day was like this for Minnijean: constantly assaulted, spat on, and insulted. But one day, after one of the assemblies, Minnijean was pushed over the edge. As she was stepping into homeroom, anticipating the relief of sitting down and getting off her bleeding heels, she heard the clack of Mary Janes behind her. She turned her head to look. *Whack!* She felt something sharp strike her head. Her ears rang. Her eyes felt heavy. She was dizzy and shaking. She looked around, only to see a white girl grinning with glee, a purse full of combination locks splayed open on the ground.

Minnijean gripped the wall for support and gritted her teeth.

Leave me alone, white trash! (Bennett, 2020)

Minnijean left the purse on the ground and walked away. Because she didn't take the purse, she had no evidence of the assault, and she was subsequently suspended indefinitely. In other words, she had been expelled.

...I didn't have any evidence of what happened. That was a good excuse to get rid of me. And after that someone sent around a card that said "One down, eight to go." (Thirteen: Media with Impact, 2009)

***

Suspension Notice

LITTLE ROCK PUBLIC SCHOOLS

Name of Pupil Brown, Minnijean *Birthdate* Sept. 11, 1941 *Grade* 11th

Name of Parent

or Guardian Mr. & Mrs. W.B. Brown

DEAR PATRON:

It becomes my duty to inform you that Minnijean Brown has been suspended from Central High School, for the following reasons:

REASONS:

Reinstated on probation January 13, 1958, with the agreement that she would not retaliate verbally or physically, to any harassment but would leave the matter to school authorities to handle.

After provocation of girl student, she called the girl "white trash", after which the girl threw her purse at Minnijean.

Very truly yours,

Principal

Source: (Smithsonian's History Explorer, 2020)

***

Minnijean and the Little Rock Nine appeared before the Supreme Court to testify about the impact of the *Brown v. Board of Education of Topeka* decision. *Brown v. Board of Education of Topeka* was a 1951 court case concerning Oliver Brown, a parent, and the public school district in Topeka, Kansas. The lawsuit was filed when Oliver Brown, a local Black resident of Topeka, was prevented from enrolling his daughter in the school that was closest to their home. He was instead told to have his daughter ride a bus to a segregated Black elementary school farther away. The Browns and twelve other families testified against the public school district, arguing that the district's segregation policy was unconstitutional.

The court ruled against Brown, using *Plessy v. Ferguson*, which is a case about segregation whose ruling stated if the facilities were equal, segregation was not in direct violation of the Fourth Amendment and therefore Constitutional, as precedent. The case was then appealed to the Supreme Court by the Brown family and NAACP Chief Counsel Thurgood Marshall, where *Plessy v. Ferguson* was overturned, and segregation was found to be unconstitutional. (Duignan, 2022; History, 2022)

In 1957, the Little Rock Nine testified in federal court to test the precedent set by *Brown v. Board of Education of Topeka*. Their years at Central High School would be used as legal evidence that the *Brown* ruling was wrong and to prevent Arkansas' governor from stopping school integration altogether. Ernest Green, and then Elizabeth Eckford, testified. The judge decided that no more testimonies were necessary.

"There is no real evidence here that we shouldn't proceed with the court-ordered integration of Central High School," the judge said. "The order is so entered." (Pattillo-Beals, 1994)

In 1958, the Little Rock Nine and their advisor, Daisy Bates, were awarded the Spingarn Medal by the NAACP—a medal awarded to "the highest or noblest achievement by a living African American during the preceding year or years in any honorable field." (The Editors of Encyclopedia Britannica, 2021)

The other members of the Little Rock Nine finished their education at Central High School with most of them going on to pursue a university education and a career in speaking (Little Rock Nine Foundation, 2022).

After being expelled from Central High School, Minnijean transferred to New Lincoln High School in Manhattan, New York. She looked around at all the sights and sounds and fell in love. The seemingly endless skyscrapers and smooth sidewalks made her feel right at home.

> *New York felt great because it was a private progressive school. In my class there were three Black girls. It was a very small school and many of the students had been there from kindergarten on. And so it turned out to be really fun because I had good friends, I got to be in the place. It was like a normal life. What I had thought maybe Central would be, just school and all the things about school that we expect in our lives. So it was amazing [...] my daughter says that the reason that I'm not wounded deeply it's because I have that experience.*

Minnijean felt a bit uneasy leaving her family to live with the Clark family—they were on the New Lincoln High school board—but putting together plays and dramas with her classmates helped put her heart at ease.

> *We wrote our own plays and wrote musicals. This is a very upscale private school. So a lot of kids of famous people. So we wrote our own plays and our own musicals. So I don't even remember, but I could be in activities. There*

were no sports to think of, thank goodness. Yeah, and I had friends, good friends. So it was great.

After graduating from New Lincoln High School, Minnijean majored in journalism at Southern Illinois University. She moved to Canada, where she received a Master of Social Work degree at Carleton University. Afterwards, she moved back to the US to work for the Clinton Administration as the deputy assistant secretary for workforce diversity at the Department of the Interior. After working in the administration for three years, she became a public speaker (Little Rock Nine Foundation, 2022).

Throughout her life, Minnijean has received a plethora of awards for her courage. She received the Lifetime Achievement Tribute by the Canadian Race Relations Foundation, an award given to those who acknowledge and honor individuals who promote the principles outlined in the Canadian Race Relations Foundation Act; the International Wolf Award, an award given to individuals, organizations, and communities in recognition of their efforts to reduce racial intolerance and to improve peace and understanding; the Spingarn Medal, an award given by the NAACP to recognize outstanding achievement by a Black person; an award from the W.E.B. DuBois Institute, which awards scholars at various stages in their careers in the fields of African and African-American studies with fellowships to facilitate the writing of doctoral dissertations. Finally, along with the other members of the Little Rock Nine, she received the Congressional Gold Medal (Little Rock Culture Vulture, 2017; Lavin, 2022).

During their time at Central High School, the Little Rock Nine went on a tour around the United States to talk to the public. On the tour, Minnijean finally found some relief. She could hang out in the main room of her tour bus without fear of being attacked. She could talk to Melba, Thelma, and Carlotta about boys and about the latest rock 'n' roll sensation: Elvis Presley. They giggled over magazines and wondered what life would be like when they were adults. Most importantly, they could just be *kids*.

The Nine tried to keep their conversations away from what was happening at school. They did this to the point where they didn't know everything that had happened until they organized a time to straighten it all out years later. However, the tour allowed them the time to talk about these things without feeling a strain on their lungs and without the fear they avoided acknowledging in the first place. Every little hesitation, the wondering if they had somehow caused the harassment they were facing, was brushed over by debates among themselves about what to wear the next day.

> *We mostly talked about other things like what are we wearing tomorrow? Do we like Elvis Presley or not? Should we like Elvis Presley? And we kept our conversations pretty much not about what was happening.*

As they toured the country, the Nine began to get a wider sense of their impact. For the first time, Minnijean realized they were coming to see *her* for being someone they considered a *hero*.

> *People were so happy to meet us and it was then that we started to see what it meant for people, what we meant and what that whole situation meant because people were so excited to meet us. As a matter of fact, they would shake our hands so hard they would hurt, and*

people just wanted to be close. So it was the beginning of seeing what it meant to other people. Because you can't see that when you're in it. And so that helped us to get a sense of how important it was to particularly Black people, but I think to all kinds of people. And the other thing that was interesting that fits with that in knowing the significance was letters we got from around the world and people just saying they helped, just wonderful letters.

Since her days as a Little Rock Nine member, Minnijean has become an enthusiastic environmentalist and climate change activist. She now lives in Canada with her grandchildren. She has been involved in an annual project named Soldier into the Past for the past twenty years, where she teaches nonviolence to over ten thousand students for a week. She does talks, mostly for schools and educational environments. In her free time, Minnijean tends to her garden.

Minnijean Brown Trickey (Image provided by SPIRIT TAWFIQ)

...*one of the things I think the mob taught me is that I would become a nonviolence activist and I continue to teach nonviolence and talk about it. And it's hard because people say, oh my God, nonviolence, look people, there are people who have the guns and the armor and the tank. You can't go up against that with what you read. You have to go against that with a strength, a purpose and commitment. [...] the young people, they're saying, no, you're phony. You're not doing this right. And we are going to call you on it. So I have a great admiration for those young people, so much.*

CHAPTER 3
1963

Girls, aged 14 to 17, in detention center in Birmingham, Alabama.
New York Daily News Archive/New York Daily News via Getty Images

NAJAH NAJIY VS. RACIAL INEQUALITY

Blood streamed down the left side of Mr. Reeves' face. His right eye, a deep shade of purple, was swollen shut. A smile quivered at the edges of his mouth as his daughter came into sight, but he couldn't hold it. *Thump.* His knees hit the doorstep.

Annie rushed to his side and squatted on her heels.

"What happened?"

"A policeman."

It happened at a party his brother was hosting. He had headed over to the party straight after church. He rarely had time to socialize between work and church responsibilities, and he had been looking forward to relaxing.

During the party, someone had suffered some sort of injury and the police were called. When officers entered the house, Mr. Reeves tried to respectfully explain what had happened. The officer struck the back of his head, slamming him onto the floor while he spat racial slurs. "Who asked you?"

> *It was devastating. This is my first time talking about it without crying. I've been interviewed on videos and all but never talked about it without being emotional about it.*

The policeman's treatment of her father came as a shock to Annie, now known as Najah Najiy. Neither her grandparents nor her father had ever discussed the treatment of their people in the Jim Crow South, opting instead to teach her the importance of love—even for those who would wrong her.

> There was never a time growing up that my grandparents taught us anything about what was going on. They didn't want to discuss those things that were going on, the hate crimes and all that. We were never taught to hate anyone. Anyone. Those people who were doing all those criminal things to our people? Nothing in our home about hate or anyone.

Annie had, of course, seen the segregation all around her, from having to drink from separate water fountains to not being allowed to swim in the downtown park's pool, to her father being constantly pulled over by white police officers. She didn't experience this regularly due to living in a Black neighborhood, but whenever she traveled outside her block, she felt the sting of hate.

Four years after Mr. Reeves came home from his brother's party, Mr. Masters—a man from the church the Reeveses attended—was scouting around Annie's neighborhood.

"There's going to be a meeting at the Sixteenth Street Baptist Church today," he said. "They're looking for people to join the Children's March with Martin Luther King. Will you come?" he asked Annie.

She glanced back at her father, who was sitting in the living room. For just a millisecond, the bruises that had long since healed seemed to reappear. She looked at Mr. Masters and nodded.

"Alright. I'll come."

> That was my motivation. I said, "This is a man I love more than anybody in the world," because I was a

> *young child seeing this man, this handsome man ... who could fight, but if he did, he would get killed, of course. He would die. He came to the door, he stood there, and I said, "What happened?" He told me what happened, and that has left an indelible print in my mind. That was my motivation for getting involved in the Civil Rights Movement.*

Annie stepped inside the church. Reverend Bevel and Reverend Abernathy stood on the stage in front of her with a crowd of about one hundred children in the pews. She took a seat on the right, close to the front.

"We're going to be holding these placards up," Reverend Bevel explained. "We are going to make our placards on a stick and walk in front of the stores." The children nodded, already thinking of slogans to put on their placards.

"But, children," Reverend Abernathy interrupted, "there is a great possibility that we will be arrested." The crowd stiffened. "If we do get arrested, there is no telling how long we'll be in there. Are you all still interested?"

The children glanced around at each other, as if having an intense, silent conversation. Annie looked up at the reverend and nodded.

"Good."

A few weeks passed. The children and reverends made their signs. They lined up outside Woolworth, placards raised high in the air. Soon, thousands of Americans from other cities joined them with signs of their own.

> ...it wasn't long before the paddy wagon came and put us in the paddy wagon. They weren't ready for us. They didn't really know that everything was sort of hush. They didn't realize that this was going to be as big as it was. People came from all over the United States to participate in the Civil Rights Movement during that time. So, they put us in the paddy wagon.

The children sat on both sides of the paddy wagon, still lined up, but sitting. Annie watched the city fly by outside the window. Everything was a blur until they reached the central jail on Sixth Avenue. The children filed upstairs to give their fingerprints. Hundreds of Mary Janes and oxford shoes clacked up the gray, concrete stairway. A chill settled in the hall as each child lined up and robotically stamped their fingerprints before getting into a separate line to be escorted to their cells. Twenty children were crammed into each cell, with the girls upstairs and the boys downstairs. The guards had taken the springs and mattresses off each of the beds. Some of the children slept on the floor, some on the bed frames, and some on springs.

Annie tossed and turned on the floor. She tried to use the crook of her arm as a pillow, but she could not sleep. This went on for hours, each position she took felt exponentially more uncomfortable than the last. She finally dozed off around 1 a.m.

A flashlight shone in Annie's eyes. "Let's go," the guard barked, waking the other children. The girls filed out of the cell.

Annie checked the clock on the wall—3 a.m. *What is going on?* The guard took them down a flight of stairs to a room with a ruler on the wall. They were getting mugshots. Each girl took one, still a bit dazed from being awakened so suddenly.

> *I remember when they took the picture, my hair was standing up on top of my head because they woke me up while I was asleep, all of us...*

After taking the mugshots, the children were given disgusting powdered eggs for breakfast.

One of the children started singing, "We Shall Overcome," and soon all the children were singing the most popular song at the time. Music and attempted harmonies echoed through the jail, hundreds of voices coming together. They sang for hours, with songs of peace and prayers—making the freezing jail cells feel a little warmer.

> *It wasn't really a bad experience in jail. It was not a bad experience because there were so many of us, you see ... we were just singing songs and we were talking about things that children talk about because, I'm sure the adults had more mature conversations, but we did not [...] Obviously, we just wanted some candy, some cookies.*

A few days after Annie arrived at the jail, her sister came in with armloads of cookies and candy. Swedish Fish, Swee-TARTS, and Lemonheads flooded onto the cell floor. The children were ecstatic.

Annie's sister had one more surprise—literally up her sleeve—just for Annie.

> It was a chocolate candy. It was so good. Candy never tasted that good before. It's because when you're hungry for something that tastes good, it's just like if someone had brought some spaghetti in there, whatever, something I love a lot, it was just delicious because we were locked up and didn't have anything.

Martin Luther King, Jr. had visited Birmingham, Alabama a few weeks prior to the march on May 2nd and May 3rd. He had already been advocating for the end of segregation through peaceful protest all over the country. However, as more and more people were arrested due to their advocacy, less and less people were able to stand with him. Determined to keep the fight for integration rolling, King decided Birmingham would be a major center for the Civil Rights Movement. Because King was a minister, he contacted multiple Black churches asking to speak to their congregations. For many children in Birmingham, King's speeches at their churches were their first exposure to his work. These speeches were the ones that inspired Mr. Masters (Clark, 2021).

King was jailed on April 16th, 1963, during the Children's Crusade. Law enforcement in Birmingham made a rule that King would no longer be allowed to organize protests in the city.

While he was imprisoned, King wrote a letter. One of the paragraphs read: "… I am in Birmingham because injustice is here. Just as the eighth-century prophets left their little villages and carried their 'thus saith the Lord' far beyond the boundaries of their hometowns; and just as the Apostle Paul left his little village of Tarsus and carried the gospel of Jesus Christ to practically every hamlet and city of the Greco-Roman world, I too am compelled to carry the gospel of freedom beyond my particular hometown. Like Paul, I must constantly respond to the Macedonian call for aid." (King, 1963)

This letter was distributed nationally, and soon almost everyone in Birmingham had read it in its entirety—except for the kids in jail.

> [Martin Luther King, Jr.] said, "I love you all," [...] "We love you too, Dr. King." He was downstairs, we were upstairs, of course. That was our only experience in hearing his voice and knowing that he was present during that time...

Although that was Annie's only experience with Dr. King, hearing he had been released from jail relatively quickly filled her with hope.

Annie continued going to protests and engaging in the Children's March after a few weeks when she was released from jail. She looked out at the crowd surrounding her and the other marchers. A lump formed in her throat, but she resisted her fear. *You can do this again, Annie. Come on...* She took a step forward, her Mary Janes clicking across the cobblestone roads. She took one step, then another. *Come on.* She raised her sign above her head with quaking hands and felt her fear turn into concentrated determination as she stared at the sea of police officers before her. She joined in the chant.

Her chest felt tight, but she didn't care. Her legs shook, but she forced them to stand firm. She remembered her friends, who had just been jailed again. *Enough.*

She glanced at the marcher beside her. They gave each other a quick nod. Thousands of children joined the march, blocking the streets and chanting for equality. The other half of the marching children had been arrested and jailed the day before. Most of the parents had also been arrested for protesting, so it was up to the kids. Cars stopped, pedestrians watched, and everyone stared as the crowd marched by. The flashes of cameras and murmurs of confusion rose from the onlookers. Some people smiled, most of them screamed, but all of them were watching.

The marches lasted for eight days. The city drew up an agreement to desegregate businesses and release every protestor from jail, but that was not all the Children's March accomplished. The March put fuel back into the Civil Rights Movement. The March inspired President John F. Kennedy to address segregation and civil rights within the law, which eventually led to the Civil Rights Act of 1964.

The Civil Rights Act banned segregation in public spaces and banned employment discrimination on the basis of race, color, religion, sex, or national origin. The Act also prohibited the use of federal funds for discriminatory programs, authorized the Department of Education to mandate school desegregation, and forbade the unequal application of voting requirements. Martin Luther King cited the Civil Rights Act as the "second emancipation," highlighting its undeniable importance. The Civil Rights Act was later expanded to include Americans with disabilities, senior citizens, and women. (History, 2010)

Annie's story does not end there. A few years after her participation in the Children's March, she joined the march from Selma to Montgomery. She was pregnant with her first child, but the determination in her heart dominated the weariness in her body. Her yellow dress fluttered gracefully at her ankles as she neared the stage. Her husband stood at her side, wearing regular clothes instead of his military uniform to avoid getting in trouble. Despite rain drenching the crowd and blurring their vision, Dr. Martin Luther King Jr. and his wife Coretta stepped up to the microphone, standing tall against the looming storm.

> *I was happy. I felt that something had to be done, and all along from seeing my dad the first time experiencing injustice, I've always felt that something had to be done. That's why I felt that I had to participate. It was very important that I participated in the movement. Whatever it had to be done that wasn't violent, I felt I needed to do that. It's just my sense of justice has always been pretty heightened all my life, really, even since I was a child. Justice. It's important. I always try to treat people the way I want to be treated because that's the way I was brought up anyway. My family taught us that, and that's the way we observed that from them. What you see, you do.*

After joining the Nation of Islam and divorcing her then-husband, Annie changed her name to Najah and became a model for her friend Kind Jay's African clothing store. One day, Jay got a call from none other than Grammy-award-winning singer Tina Turner. Her backup dancers were being harassed at the hotel she and her crew were staying at, so she called Kind Jay to help get her voice out there. Kind Jay asked Najah to come with him and introduced her to Turner.

> [Tina Turner] wasn't acting like she was that important or anything because she was from Mississippi or somewhere, Tennessee or somewhere. She was just a Southern girl, just down-to-earth, approachable. That was that experience being in the hotel—and you [couldn't] be in the hotel lobby and Black, so that was quite an experience.

Najah went on to attend Black Panther meetings before marching in her new city of Los Angeles.

> So, we marched there ... [the slogan was] "Free Ruchell. Ruchell Magee. Free Ruchell. Free all political prisoners. Free Fleeta Drumgo. Free Michelle. Free all political prisons." I sure remember that slogan. It was one other person that we were chanting. ... My daughters, there are pictures with them with the raised fists. They were getting involved in the movement too. They were young kids. What made me really stop getting involved ... That was a riot in Vegas. My two daughters, at that time, they were throwing with those smoke devices around the cars. I said, "I don't want [my children] to be in danger," so I had to stop participating in riots. I mean, I wasn't participating in it, but I was in the crowd and had my children with me. I didn't want anything to happen to them because they could get shot. If they got shot and I didn't, I could never forgive myself for that.

Although Najah stopped attending marches and demonstrations, her work did not stop there. She has been featured in movies and music videos mainly around the subject of civil rights. She became an actress and got into African dance and drumming. She went on to complete her teaching degree at the University of California Los Angeles (UCLA), and she still teaches today. She teaches chess, African dance, and drumming. She enjoys occasional visits from the children she fostered over the course of fifteen years. After retiring from teaching, she became a licensed spiritual practitioner at Agape International Spiritual Center and now works on the prayer line.

Najah Najiy (Image provided by Najah Najiy)

The sun knows it's supposed to shine. There are clouds that will pass the sun, but the sun is still shining even though a cloud will pass it. The sun is still shining. We always love even though something happens to us that is horrible. We can't allow that to put our light out. We can continue shining our light brightly. [...] Don't waste your time discriminating against anyone. Love, peace, joy, living. My life is good. My life is so good. Seventy-seven years old. My life is so good because no matter what happens, I see the good, I see the lesson in it for me to grow, for me to be better, whatever it is.

CHAPTER 4
1969

Bettmann/Bettmann via Getty Images

MARY BETH TINKER VS. CENSORSHIP

Explosions echoed on the television. *Boosh!*

Mary Beth had seen many news programs about the Vietnam War, but she was still deeply disturbed every evening as she and her family watched the TV news hosted by Walter Cronkite. Often cited as "the most trusted man in America," Walter Cronkite had a good reputation among Americans because of his impartial reporting on World War II and now the Vietnam War.

But there had been another man besides Walter Cronkite who Mary Beth and her family trusted for news about the growing Vietnam War and that was her father, Leonard Tinker. He was a Methodist minister, but now he worked as a peace education secretary for the American Friends Service Committee. For that, he traveled through five states teaching people about the Vietnam War and encouraging a peaceful solution.

Sometimes, Mary Beth got to accompany him, setting out brochures and booklets about Vietnam. She felt proud to help her father teach people about Vietnam and encourage peace, not war.

The USA's involvement in Vietnam had begun in 1950, as the Vietnamese fought a war of independence against their colonizers, the French. Because the independence leaders identified as Communists, some government officials in the US were afraid Vietnam would become Communist, and they started sending support to the French. But it didn't matter because the Vietnamese won their war of independence against the French in 1954.

After that, the US government supported the division of Vietnam into North and South, with the communist government in the north and a US-backed government in the south. They began to send even more US soldiers to try to stop the government of the north.

By the time the war ended in 1975, 58,220 US soldiers were killed—making it one of the bloodiest wars in US history—and 3 to 4 million Vietnamese were also killed. (National Archives, 2008; Britannica, 2020)

But back in 1965, ten years earlier, Mary Beth was getting more and more disturbed about the shocking news about Vietnam: huts burning, "body bags" on the ground, and children running in terror from the bombs. She and a small group of students in Des Moines, Iowa, decided to wear black armbands to school to mourn the dead and support a truce.

Two years before, she and others in Des Moines had worn black armbands to mourn four little Black girls in Birmingham, Alabama, who were killed when their church was bombed by white supremacists. This time, the armbands would be for US and Vietnamese soldiers.

Mary Beth Tinker wearing a black armband to mourn the girls killed in the Sixteenth Street Church bombing (Image provided by Mary Beth Tinker)

> *The war and the nightly report and then there was the body count, you know- Walter Cronkite, he would give his body count, and it was all just horrific.*

"I don't know if you kids should be wearing those armbands," Mary Beth's father said to her and her brother John. "You know the principal's just passed a rule against wearing them."

"But Dad," John said. "You taught us to stand up for what we believe and for peace."

John Tinker, 1969 (Image provided by Mary Beth Tinker)

Still, John decided to wait a day or two to try to change the principal's mind.

But Mary Beth had already left for Warren Harding Jr. High School, where she was in eighth grade. When she got there, nothing was out of the ordinary. Students and teachers acted as they always did, until Mary Beth got to her math class. Her teacher was waiting at the door with a pink slip and telling her to go to the office.

She walked to the office slowly, nervous and scared. She hadn't really been in trouble before, and she didn't know what would happen when she got there. At the office the vice principal, asked her to sit down, and he asked her to take off the armband because it was against the rules.

Looking around the office, Mary Beth got even more nervous and then took off the armband. "Whew,' she thought as she headed back to class. "I'm glad that's over." But it wasn't over.

In a few minutes, someone came to the door of the math class and asked Mary Beth to return to the office. There, she was asked to come into the office of the Girls Advisor.

"You've broken the rules, Mary Beth, by wearing the armband, so I'm going to have to suspend you." More nervous than ever, Mary Beth took the suspension paper and walked out the front door of the school. Three other students were suspended from another high school—Roosevelt High School—that day, and the next day, her brother, John, was suspended from North High School.

> *My parents were [understanding of the suspension] eventually. My mom was for sure, and then my dad, we convinced him, because he hadn't originally thought we should wear the armbands because it was against the rules... but we were able to convince him in the end.*

The five students who were suspended and their parents met with the American Civil Liberties Union (ACLU), who agreed to take their case to court. But first, the ACLU said, the students would have to try to get the school board to change the rule.

Two big school board meetings were held, and many people were emotional on both sides. But in the end, the rule against armbands remained in place.

> *...mostly [the harassment] was right around the time that we wore the armbands. People threatened to bomb our house on Christmas Eve, and they threw red paint at our house. They called us communists, sent us threatening mail that had a hammer and sickle on it, and said "hate," and called us traitors, some people. A lady called me on the phone and said, "I'm going to kill you."*

No matter what they did, the Tinkers couldn't get a break. They lost in the US District Court in Iowa. They appealed, but the vote ended in a tie. With nowhere else to go, the Tinkers had no choice but to appeal to the Supreme Court.

***

Mary Beth looked around her. The hair on the back of her neck stood up as she stood in the chilly courthouse hallway. She stared at the men in suits and ties, pacing in and out of rooms, each with an unimpressed scowl and an eye on their watch. Mary Beth could almost count the rhythm of their footsteps combined—like a high school marching band routine.

She wrapped her arms around herself, suddenly conscious of her small stature under the looming gazes of passersby. Her fingers tingled as she forced a smile onto her face when making eye contact. Her smile twitched.

"Come on, then," said her lawyer, Dan Johnston, paying no mind to the swarm of suits surrounding them. "We have to get there before our time on the docket!" Mary Beth nodded slowly and followed behind him, dragging her feet and wishing she would become part of the floor. She wasn't completely convinced by Johnston's words, but they were all she had at the moment.

As Mary Beth settled into her seat, she was hit with a wave of worry. She couldn't focus on any one thing. From the blood-red curtains to the freezing wooden chairs, to the luminescent candelabras, everything was too bright, too sharp, and too much. She buried her head in her hands, wondering if this was the right choice after all. *Will my teachers hate me? What comes next? What if we lose again? Can I handle another hearing?* Sitting in the icy chair next to her brother, father, mother, and a friend, Mary Beth's mind finally became still. *We have to win this. We deserve this. If we lose, then I guess we lose.*

"... *Tinker v. the Des Moines Independent Community School District*," the judge bellowed, "is now being heard."

***

The ruling came shortly after. The Tinkers had won, setting a precedent for student free speech for the foreseeable future. Even today, the Tinker case is used to determine the outcome of free speech cases (ACLU, 2022; see *Chapter 11: Brandi Levy*).

***

After winning her case, Mary Beth Tinker continued her education and became a pediatric nurse. She held a master's degree in both public health and nursing. In 2013, Mary Beth started "Tinker Tours" with student rights attorney Mike Hiestand. "Tinker Tours" is a national speaker series featuring speakers promoting youth activism and youth rights. Mary Beth Tinker personally spoke to more than twenty thousand students and teachers at fifty-eight stops, including schools, colleges, churches, a youth detention facility, courts, and several national conventions (Tinker Tours, 2022).

In 2006, the ACLU National Board of Directors' Youth Affairs Committee—the same organization that represented her at the Supreme Court—renamed their annual youth affairs award the "Mary Beth Tinker Youth Involvement Award." (ACLU Iowa, n.d.)

> ...there are also many moments in my adult years since then—when students talk about the things they are speaking up about, and that they are using their

rights to speak up about. Today, I had a very good moment when a high school girl wrote to me after I gave a talk to her class by video yesterday in Ohio, and she said how comforting it was to hear the story and to know about other kids who speak up and stand up for things. That was a very wonderful moment, and I'm very privileged to have many moments like that with young people today.

Mary Beth Tinker still conducts speaking tours at the time of this writing and actively participates in union activism. At the moment, her two joys are growing kale in her backyard and gardening with other members of her community.

I am a retired nurse. A nurse practitioner. I spend half my time speaking with students and teachers in groups, in classes, about our case and about the rights of young people. And the other half of my time I spend in food justice and urban agriculture. And I love to grow healthy, organic crops at the local public college where we have a group that is working on food justice issues. We have a huge community garden. I love to get out in nature, and I hope that all the students will spend time in nature too because it's very healing, and we need to help the earth and to help heal the earth and all of its creatures, including ourselves.

When I compare my case to Mary Beth's, I see some similarities and key differences. While Mary Beth had to fight her school, my school was almost entirely supportive. However, we both had to grow up quickly. Mary Beth and I were both thirteen and in the eighth grade when our cases began. Even so, we stood up for what we believed in and didn't back down in the face of adversity.

> ...take heart and know that you're connected with people throughout this country and throughout the world who are speaking up and working towards a better world—a world of peace and justice—and that you should take care of yourselves and each other. Know that it's a good way of life to speak up for changing things that are not fair, that are not right. And that it's a meaningful, good way of life. It's a very rewarding way of life.

Mary Beth Tinker, age thirteen; 1969 (Image provided by Mary Beth Tinker)

CHAPTER 5
1980

Available from: Aaron Fricke

AARON FRICKE VS. HOMOPHOBIA

New York, New York, Aaron thought. The drama class buzzed inside the school bus as they took in the skyscrapers that towered over them. It was three months into the school year.

They don't have buildings like this in Rhode Island. Brightly lit billboards and flashy advertisements surrounded the drama students of Cumberland High School. The blinding lights twinkled in Aaron's eyes, but his mind was far removed from the Broadway production they were about to see.

Paul was a grade above Aaron. When Paul tried to bring his boyfriend to prom, the school would not allow it. The school principal, Richard Lynch, prevented Paul from bringing his date to prom. Paul attempted to sue the school, but being seventeen, he needed parental approval. Paul didn't end up getting parental approval and was thrown out of his home.

> *So [Paul]'s in New York city on his own, making it fine, or at least he's not on the streets, but still he was struggling to get by. I mean, was not expecting to have to be on the streets. He expected to have a senior year in high school, but it didn't happen that way.*

A month before Aaron's trip to New York, Mr. Lynch called an assembly to address what had happened with Paul as a way of discouraging students from trying something similar.

> *It was being spun as though Paul, he was wrong, that gay people had no right to attend prom. And I just knew at that point, I felt as though I saw the cause*

and effect of the homophobia that I had experienced. I was eighteen at this point and I saw it, it was like the students went crazy, went wild with applause like this year we're going to have a great prom not like last year [...] And so I knew something had to be done. I knew that it was wrong. It pissed me off.

It was on this trip to New York that Aaron decided to pay Paul a visit for some counsel.

Aaron pounded his fist into his palm and frowned. "We have to fight this," he said. Paul looked up as a big, broad smile slowly spread across his face. A mischievous twinkle appeared in his eye, and he threw back his head and laughed, rocking back and forth, and holding his stomach. Aaron waited for him to calm down.

"No, I'm serious about this," he said when Paul stopped laughing.

Paul's face dropped. "I don't know," Paul said, looking up at the ceiling.

Aaron sat down next to Paul on the couch. "It's got to be done. I mean, we've got to at this point."

Paul stared at the floor, stone-faced. "It's been a *year*, Aaron."

"What they did to you was wrong."

"Yes! It was. But I'm not *there* anymore. I'm ready to move on."

"But they're *continuing* to do it."

"Aaron—"

"Look, school dances aren't really my scene. You know that. But *I* know you loved the dances. You should've been able to have your night, but you didn't. We've got a chance here. We've got to take it."

Paul looked at Aaron and managed a weak smile. "Okay."

Aaron smiled. "Here's my plan."

"Lay it on me."

"I'm going to ask Lynch if he'd let a gay couple go to prom together." Paul blinked. "I'm just going to ask and see what he says."

> *...it was when I went to New York with our school for drama class, to go to Broadway, a Broadway show. And we went to see Paul [...] So yeah, that was in New York. And then we talked it out and I said, "I'm just going to ask and see what [Mr. Lynch] says."*

***

"No, I wouldn't," Lynch said, hands clasped on his desk.

Aaron let out a small sigh. *Called it.* "Okay, thank you, bye," Aaron said. He wheeled around, slapped his knees and marched out of the office.

> *...surprise, surprise, he said, 'No.' And I remember I just wheeled around and I knew he was going to say*

that and just walked right out. I didn't even say a word to him about it. I said, 'Okay, thank you. Bye.'

***

"He said no, Paul." Aaron rolled his eyes.

"We knew he would," said Paul, almost chuckling.

"I'm still going to prom."

"I thought you said prom wasn't your thing?"

"Well, I *have* to *now*." Aaron spread his hands. "It's a challenge!"

> ...from there, then I started making calls. I mean, Paul had given me the name of a couple of people who had helped him the year before. And it's funny because I remember back after the prom and during the prom period time there were people saying that I had been paid to do this because of Paul's case the year before, and that this is all just a preconceived thing by the gay movement. And there was none of that, it was just me. I mean, not even Paul was on board at first. And when I really explored the bottom individual intricacies of it, it really was just largely sticking up for a friend, just saying, "That's not right."

***

Aaron decided to ask his parents for permission to sue the school. He knew he didn't need their permission because he was already eighteen years old, but something didn't seem right about not asking his parents for at least their opinion. Aaron toed into the living room.

> ...they were in the midst of a divorce and it was all so much emotional turmoil because my mother was throwing my father out, had served him papers and he was either not supposed to be in the house or he had just come back to get his things, to leave, to go. [...] I asked because I had said at the time I thought if they said no that I wouldn't do it. I don't know why I thought that, but I did.

Aaron took a deep breath and took another step into the living room. *If Dad says not to, I'm not going to sue. I'm not. I'm just—just tell them already.*

"Mom, Dad." Aaron stood tall, head up, and jaw nervously clenched. "I'm going to sue Cumberland."

Aaron's mom shrugged, surprised at being interrupted, "You can do what you want, you're eighteen years old."

"You're your own man," Aaron's father added, gesturing vaguely at Aaron. "Do what you want to." Aaron was surprised to feel his heart sink. Aaron looked at his parents and nodded, walking out of the room.

There's no turning back now. I'm going to sue.

***

When Aaron told his father he was gay, the man dropped to his knees and burst into tears. Aaron rushed to console him.

"It'll be alright, I promise..."

> ...when I told him that I was gay what he did, he cried. I mean, he cried his eyes out in a way that I've never seen him or any really adult man cry. I mean, it wasn't like boohoo. But it was like literally the tears came flooding. [...] And it wasn't, are you sure or anything like that, it was just right away crying.

It took Aaron and his father a while to heal and reconfigure their perceptions of each other. But, once they reunited, they decided to write a book together to explain their experiences.

***

After getting his parents' permission, Aaron filed the lawsuit with the organization GLAD. Aaron and his attorneys requested a preliminary injunction, submitting the following opinion:

> Most of the time, a young man's choice of a date for the senior prom is of no great interest to anyone other than the student, his companion, and, perhaps, a few of their classmates. But in Aaron Fricke's case, the school authorities actively disapprove of his choice, the other students are upset, the community is abuzz, and out-of-state newspapers consider the matter newsworthy. [...] All this fuss arises because Aaron Fricke's intended escort

> is another young man. Claiming that the school's refusal to allow him to bring a male escort violates his first and fourteenth amendment rights, Fricke seeks a preliminary injunction ordering the school officials to allow him to attend with a male escort. (Fricke v. Lynch, 1980)

The court eventually ruled in Aaron's favor, not only granting him the right to take a male date to prom, but also forcing the school to provide enough security so Aaron and his date wouldn't have to worry about retaliation.

***

Aaron ended up going to the prom with a male date—his friend, Paul.

***

Now, Aaron lives with his partner and his two cats. He has written a multitude of books, some co-authored with his father.

When explaining his philosophy, Aaron frequently returns to a memory of a family vacation in June. That was the first time he ever witnessed a pride parade. He was eight or nine years old at the time, and he had never really been told about gay people in his small Rhode Island town, but since the paraders were shouting slogans, he knew what was going on. He saw signs, floats, and brightly colored costumes. That memory has remained in his mind and informed him of the sense of community he wanted to feel a part of.

Aaron Fricke, 1980 (Image provided by Aaron Fricke)

I know in my book when they read it, I always hope that they came away with the feeling that they're not alone [...] I know that that's true, even now there are a lot of gay people who feel alone. [...] Or it's okay to be scared actually. It's okay to look out and see. [...] though my book was written in 1981, it makes it very timely in that I think that kids today can feel the same way. I mean, be watching all this parade of gay characters go by, but they go by, and it's like you're not part of them and you don't know how to be part of them. And if you have someone whispering in your ear, these are bad people. And I know that there are still people that do that to their kids, maybe less so than before, but it happens and those people are going to feel more alone than ever. I think that's my target audience. So that's what I want to be, who I want to be speaking to is those people that feel scared and alone.

CHAPTER 6
1988

Courtesy of Gallaudet Archives

BRIDGETTA BOURNE-FIRL VS. ABLEISM AGAINST DEAF PEOPLE

The blinding headlights of police cars bounced off brightly painted signs: "DEAF PRESIDENT NOW," they read. Teachers stood with their arms crossed, blocking the exits of the school. Someone screamed. Bridgetta leaped onto the hood of a car in a fury, her hands raised in the air.

"*Deaf. President. Now!*" she screamed in American Sign Language, signing "Now" over and over in unison with the crowd.

The administration stood still in the middle of the courtyard, frozen in the students' flashlight beams. There wasn't a way out. The administrators looked around. The night sky became an illuminated gray mass as sparklers and flashlights were held aloft. The stars were outshone. The moon provided a spotlight. Cars were blocked. Traffic stopped as students from Gallaudet and other universities filled the streets, all screaming and signing at the top of their lungs. More students leapt on top of cars. A series of cheers erupted as the school was surrounded. Fire roared in spurts, effigies disintegrating as the students looked on.

In 1988, Gallaudet University—a university specifically designed for deaf students—needed to appoint a new president of their school board. At the time, the administrators overlooked the highly qualified, deaf candidates, in favor of hiring an underqualified hearing president. This sent the students into mass protests that lasted for a consecutive three days.

Each night, the protest only grew more intense: more fire, more screams, more allies. Students took to the local news to protest, gaining national traction. Every channel was filled with the faces of the Gallaudet student body screaming at the tops of their lungs. People outside Gallaudet joined the fight, making a total count of twenty thousand protestors.

> *At the conclusion of [Deaf President Now], the four of us [organizers] being young couldn't have foreseen what an impact DPN would have.* —Bridgetta Bourne-Firl

On the eighth day of the Deaf President Now movement, a swarm of students rushed toward the Field House on Gallaudet's campus, signing "We won! We won!" When the student body reached the inside of the Field House, Bridgetta and the three other student leaders were already there standing on a table, signing victoriously.

> *As the four leaders took turns signing loudly "WE WON! WE GOT THE DEAF PRESIDENT," I took pictures of every angle I could think of, chasing everyone's face. Then they said, "WE WILL MEET OUR NEW GALLAUDET PRESIDENT AT THE EMBASSY ROW HOTEL! OUR NEW DEAF PRESIDENT IS I. KING JORDAN!" Everyone was rushing and running out of the gym to go to the hotel.* —Yoon Lee, In Their Own Words, 2022

Yoon Lee was the student photographer for Gallaudet University and had been working tirelessly throughout the protests to document the events.

> *I was totally speechless and I felt like I was dreaming because you saw Deaf students, teachers, children, and parents chanting "Deaf President Now"*

every minute in the front of the campus entrance. After watching them for seven days, I felt their signs grow louder and louder. When I first heard their deaf voices, I was embarrassed by what hearing people might think. Remember, I had just transferred three months before. —Yoon Lee, In Their Own Words, 2022

Students celebrate the appointment of the first deaf president of Gallaudet University. Bettmann/Bettmann via Getty Images

Yoon's work during the DPN movement later led him to a successful film career after graduation, producing documentaries such as *Deaf People in China* and *Tomorrow Dad Still Deaf* (California State University, 2005).

After graduating from Gallaudet University with a master's degree in public administration and supervision and a bachelor's degree in American government and politics, Bridgetta became the chair of the Community Advisory Council at the California School for the Deaf-Fremont. She then became the Coordinator of Individualized Education Plans (IEP) at the Maryland School for the Deaf.

After graduation, Bridgetta went backpacking with three of her classmates across Europe.

> *While we were traveling in Europe, we would often run into deaf people who, when they realized we were Gallaudet students, would tell us how empowering DPN was for Deaf people all over the world.*
> —Bridgetta Bourne-Firl, (DPN Undocumented Voices of Women Leaders, 2019)

Bridgetta and her friends had no idea the story of DPN had reached international waters.

Bridgetta and Yoon's stories are shining examples of how protest can lead to major change. Even today, Gallaudet University has a 60 percent majority of deaf members on its school board. None of the protestors were ever penalized.

This story was inspiring to me during my case because of its emphasis on community. The story of the Deaf President Now (DPN) movement reminded me of all the people who came to the Zoning Board Association to support me with signs and chants and matching pins. DPN is a prime example of how change is made: people coming together to form their own community and fight injustice.

Courtesy of Gallaudet Archives; Bridgetta Bourne-Firl, second from the left

Deep down in my heart, […] I felt "fire" and angry because I just couldn't bear to accept in my head or heart that deaf people couldn't do things for themselves. When we were victorious, I felt like I had a new freedom and spirit. —Yoon Lee, In Their Own Words, 2022

PART 2

2000s - 2010s

CHAPTER 7
2010

Rogelio V. Solis/AP/Shutterstock.com

CONSTANCE MCMILLEN VS. HOMOPHOBIA

The senior prom, a much-anticipated event for many, was right around the corner. Excited whispers echoed through the halls, with talk of dresses, tuxes, dates, and who would be going with whom. Posters covered the walls: "PROM 2010!"

In the vice principal's office, the clamoring in the halls a muffled din, a girl sat across from the desk as the vice principal stared at her. Her hands trembled as she pressed them together, waiting for his response. She tapped her foot nervously as her stomach fluttered.

The vice principal bristled. "Constance, bringing your girlfriend to prom is not allowed."

"But—"

The vice principal sighed. "You and your girlfriend can go if y'all both bring a boy as your dates—" the principal rose from his seat "—but there would be no slow dancing, no holding hands, and no kissing between you and your girlfriend. If I see *any* of that, y'all will be kicked out. Do you understand?"

Constance nodded solemnly and trudged out of the office (*Clips 6*, 2010).

A few months later, Constance asked for permission to wear a tuxedo to prom. Her request was once again rejected, and she was told she wouldn't be allowed in if she wore a tux. (TheEllenShow, 2010)

> ...it [was] a big deal because [I was] asking permission. I shouldn't have to ask permission, but because I'm asking permission, you're going to tell me no.

This was not the first time Itawamba Agricultural High School had prevented people from attending prom. The year before, a student named June had enrolled at Itawamba after attending a school in Indiana, making her the new girl. June frequently wore stilettos, makeup, and hoop earrings to school—like many other girls at Itawamba. However, the school and a handful of June's peers took issue for one reason: June was transgender.

For the students, this was all new. In their small Texas town, they had never met a transgender person before. Their shock quickly died down, and they arrived at acceptance. However, the school administration was not as quick to back off. As the school year went on, the harassment only got worse. June was sent home multiple times, and she was eventually suspended for wearing feminine clothing.

Something has to be done, Constance thought. The next day, she rallied thirty other students to protest. They met during lunch, hunched over a single lunch table, and the plan was set.

> We had organized a protest with about thirty people and all of them dressed in our [...] brothers' clothes, females, and with no makeup on, our hair in ponytails, hats on, boots on, everything [...] we felt like what they were doing to June was wrong, and so we were gonna show up all dressed outside of our character...

The superintendent marched over. "Ladies, what do you think you're doing?" He turned to Constance. "Well, Constance? You're kind of the spokesperson for everyone here."

Constance shrugged. "It's the same thing as June wearing heels and makeup. It's wrong for y'all to ban June and not ban us."

The superintendent loomed over Constance. "Y'all are gonna go back to class. If you wanna leave, then you gotta call your parents to leave."

> Well, that day, I called the WTVA [News] [...] I had called my aunt, and my aunt had told me about this law professor at Ole' Miss that I could get in touch with. So, I did and they were like, "Well, you know, the ACLU could help June."

The next day, Constance called the ACLU and spoke with a representative. Constance explained everything, from June's suspension to the superintendent sending all the protestors home. The representative was quiet for a few moments before they replied. "Do you know that that's discrimination?"

"Yes."

The ACLU rep thought for a moment. "Has your school done anything else discriminatory?"

> And so I told them about the flyer I had seen in previous years saying, "No same-sex dates are allowed." So I was like, "I felt like that was kinda discriminatory," and they [were] like, "Well, actually, you know, your school doesn't have a right to do that. It's a violation of your Constitutional rights."

That same day, Constance and June signed for the ACLU to send a demand letter on their behalf. The letter indicated a deadline for the school's response, and if they didn't respond, Constance would sue. The school responded by canceling the prom entirely.

The ACLU filed a lawsuit on Constance's behalf to request a preliminary injunction, which would force the school to host a prom inclusive of Constance. The district court acknowledged that Constance's rights had been violated, but due to the reassurances of the school board that a private prom had already been organized by parents, denied the injunction. The school board asserted that all junior and senior students would be allowed to attend this prom, but Constance was never granted any official details, and the board members never clarified whether same-sex couples would be permitted to attend as a date. (N.D. Miss. 2010)

Constance began to receive an influx of angry texts and Facebook messages, mostly blaming her for the prom being canceled and wishing she were dead. Her classmates, friends she had known since birth, left her. (ACLU, 2010)

Nevertheless, Constance tried to be strong and attempted to buy a ticket to the prom promised in the hearing. However, shortly after Constance tried to buy a ticket, she was informed the prom had been canceled because the parent organizers didn't want to be sued for not allowing same-sex couples at the private prom. (ACLU of San Diego & Imperial Properties, 2010)

The day after the cancellation was announced, Constance was told by the administration that yet another prom had been organized by the school, one that anyone—including Constance and her girlfriend—could attend. Constance was aware that some parents were trying to organize a new prom, but when she had asked a classmate if she was invited to the parent-organized prom, she was told the school-organized prom was the only one actually happening. Constance figured the parents organizing a new prom had either been a rumor, or they didn't execute in time—and she wouldn't have to worry about it.

The "prom" organized by the school was held at the Fulton Country Club. When Constance and her date arrived, only five other students were there. The decorations were dismal, and the sound system was barely functional.

> When we pulled up, the police officers were there and then there were also people who were supportive meeting me outside. I didn't really know what to expect. And then I walked in and when I realized that no one was there, it was just like, wow, you know what I'm saying? To what extreme are you fixing to go as an adult to ostracize a child and to teach your children that it's okay to ostracize people that are different than you, that believe differently than you, that have different cultures than you do, that identify different than you understand. "We're just going to separate you. And we're going to tell this person that there's a whole 'nother prom and they're going to go there as adults. This is something that we're going to do." And that to me was just baffling. I couldn't believe what was really going down was going down.

Students who attended the parent-organized prom posted photos of the event on their Facebook pages, but many of the photos were deleted after the story became public. Some students said the event was not a prom but a birthday party, while others said it was just a private party. However, while publicly claiming the event was not a prom, students uploaded photos to their Facebook pages labeled as "Prom 2010" and posted status updates which referred to the gathering as "prom."

The harassment grew exponentially, and Constance moved to Murrah High School in Jackson, Mississippi—over two hundred miles from Itawamba County.

Eventually, the school district reached a settlement. They agreed to create a policy protecting students from discrimination on the basis of sexual orientation and gender identity, and they have since upheld their end of the deal. Constance had won (ACLU, 2010).

Constance received offers to go on a variety of talk shows as well as numerous screenplay options during the case. Dan Savage, a relationship advice columnist and podcast host, urged his followers to protest the school's decision to exclude Constance from prom. Constance was a guest on *The Ellen Show*, and Ellen DeGeneres awarded her a thirty-thousand-dollar scholarship (*TheEllenShow*, 2010).

Arriving at the Hyatt Regency Century Plaza, Constance posed in front of the orange backdrop for the GLAAD Media Awards in the tuxedo she had planned to wear for prom with the phrase "NO H8" painted on her cheek. She looked up at the iridescent purple curtains behind the glossy podium and the glass chandelier. She took a breath. She was ready. Constance walked out on stage and received a kiss on the cheek from both hosts (*GLAAD*, 2010).

"I'm really grateful that the court ruled that my rights were being violated, but I mean, I'm still sad that my school decided to cancel prom," she began. "What I hope is that high school students across the country understand that, whether you're gay or straight, you have the right to bring your date to prom." Applause resounded through the room. "Your schools should not be allowed to discriminate against you, but if they won't change, you have to speak up." (*GLAAD*, 2010)

Wanda Sykes personally invited Constance to present the Stephen F. Kolzack Award to Wanda, and she provided Constance with a vacation in Los Angeles free of expense. Constance was subsequently invited to celebrity blogger Perez Hilton's exclusive birthday party, where she was treated like a "homecoming queen for a day." (*Perez Hilton*, 2010)

Rainbow-colored confetti littered the streets at the 2010 New York City Gay Pride March. Balloon bouquets floated in every marcher's hand. Flags and banners and rainbow capes fluttered in the wind as Constance McMillen marched along, wearing a fluorescent rainbow sash over her black dress that read, "Grand Marshal." Her hair was tied half-up-half-down, and her silver eyeshadow sparkled in the New York City sun. She waved to everyone as she passed, brandishing a rainbow rose. (On Top Magazine, 2010)

> *I think [my favorite part of being the Grand Marshal was] just the walk [...] 'cause you know, you're riding*

through and you're in a car, and you're waving at everybody. [...] that day, we won because we were happy to be us and we were helping other people be happy to be them. [...] And we were all celebrating our happiness that we have found ourselves, and that we were living our best life, our true life. [...] So, it was amazing, it was very awesome. I would recommend it.

***

Constance and I both had to deal with the role reversals that our cases presented: adults acting like children and children assuming adult roles. Another common factor is setting precedents to ensure such discriminatory behaviors never happen again.

Constance McMillen (Rogelio V. Solis/AP/Shutterstock.com)

Establishing laws can take years of multiple cases to ensure progress. But, in the end, I think most of us would agree preserving civil rights is worth every minute.

Now, Constance is preparing to become a lawyer. She wants to do research as a lawyer and bring her findings before Congress to create positive change. Constance's story inspired the Broadway musical *The Prom*.

> *...at the end of the day, if you feel like something is an injustice to you or to someone around you, whether it's your friend or not, you should definitely speak your piece. And you never know what kind of knowledge you can share with people by just showing courage. You never realize how big of an impact you can make just from one small conversation that was started in a principal's office.*

CHAPTER 8
2012

M. Spencer Green/AP/Shutterstock

MARY KATE CALLAHAN VS. ABLEISM IN SPORTS

When she was five years old, a virus called transverse myelitis attacked Mary Kate's spinal cord—paralyzing her legs and affecting her core. She began swimming as a part of physical therapy, and she decided to join her local swim club. She rose to the top of the swim club and, only three *years* after she joined, became the team captain (National Women's History Museum, 2022).

The coach sighed, planting her feet on the pool deck. "You can't go to sectionals,"

"What are you talking about? I did *great* in regionals—"

The coach held up her hand and shook her head. "I know, I know." The coach looked down at Mary Kate. "But the association says your times don't qualify you."

"I'm one of the best adaptive swimmers *in Illinois*—"

"I know. But the IHSA doesn't have an adaptive swimming section and says they can't accommodate you. Apparently, they've been refusing to include athletes with disabilities for years—it's out of my hands."

Mary Kate glared at the swimming coach's back as she walked away. Jaw clenched, she gripped the cold, metal bench and began to think. *We have to fight this.*

> *I was this wide-eyed fifteen-year-old because I was lucky. I grew up never being bullied because of my, because of being in a wheelchair [...] but I think it was at that moment that it was the first time in my*

life that I realized that people do look at people with disabilities in a different way [...] I was shocked and I was surprised. But I think like the fighter in me and the determination in me also just lit up in that moment because it was like, "I'm not gonna let you get away with this."

***

A few weeks after the coach informed her that she didn't qualify for sectionals, then-high-school-sophomore Mary Kate organized a meeting with the Illinois High School Sports Association (IHSA). She sat across a big board table from a cluster of IHSA board members. Coaches, staff members and Mary Kate's parents sat next to her. The conference room walls were blindingly white, and a faint breeze of air conditioning washed over everyone. Mary Kate was the only kid. One of the IHSA members spread their hands, brushing the edge of their suit jacket sleeves on the table. They took a breath.

"You're not an athlete," they began, "because you have a disability."

Mary Kate froze.

I think that's the moment that sparked this, like, fire inside of me, because I knew I never wanted to hear those words again, but more importantly, I didn't want another child to have to hear those words again.

***

On a live video feed, Mary Kate watched her teammates walking to the edge of the deck and jumping into the cool, qualifier waters. She sighed. She rolled into the living room, stone-faced. Mary Kate put on her brakes, knit her hands together, and turned to her mother.

"I'm going to sue them."

"The IHSA? Are you sure?" Mary Kate nodded again. Mary Kate's mom relaxed her face. "Alright, let's do it."

> ...we were asking the Illinois High School Sports Association to adopt qualifying standards so athletes with disabilities had the opportunity to try to qualify for the state championship meet. [...] prior to the case, there were no qualifying standards that took into consideration that people did have physical disabilities. [...] our ask wasn't that they would just send anyone who had a physical disability to the state championship, we wanted these athletes to have to qualify and earn their right to be there.

It took the Callahans a few months to find a firm that would take their case. They eventually found Equip for Equality, a firm specifically dedicated to furthering disability rights. They filed a federal discrimination lawsuit against the Illinois High School Association (IHSA) in 2012.

The case was settled two years later. By that time, Mary Kate was a senior in high school and the captain of her school's swim team. The court sided with Mary Kate, and the IHSA agreed to:

- Have four swimming events for students with disabilities
- Create a new wheelchair division for track and field
- Modify qualifying standards for swimming/diving, track/field
- Change the terms and conditions so that student athletes with disabilities can earn points for their teams
- Create new policies and practices for accommodations
- Appoint an [Americans with Disabilities Act] coordinator to review all accommodation requests (Equip for Equality, 2018)

> *IHSA has not promulgated rules that would permit athletes with disabilities to score points in interscholastic meets—in fact, according to the plaintiffs, IHSA has explicitly refused to do so—and its regulations prohibit member schools from setting their own standards or scoring systems for athletes with disabilities [...] As a result, students who have disabilities that prevent them from meeting existing state qualifying standards are denied the opportunity to compete in IHSA-run state championship meets. Yet IHSA itself has provided different qualifying standards for state championship meets based on gender, school size, and geography, which has resulted in multiple qualifying standards for state championship meets in every event within a sport.* —The federal court ruling on Mary Kate's case (Sports Litigation Alert, 2012)

The case was settled a few weeks before the next sectional swim meet, where Mary Kate was finally able to compete.

As she looked over at her teammates swimming laps, she noted nine of them, including herself, had disabilities. A stark increase from being the only swimmer with a disability on her team. The crowd rose to their feet in a sudden standing ovation, just as it had with the completely able-bodied teams. Mary Kate smiled.

"Callahan, you're up!" the coach yelled. Mary Kate nodded and made her way over to the pool. She hit the water, speeding through the chlorinated waves, eyes trained on the nearing wall. *Pamph!* Mary Kate pushed off of the wall and refocused on the block. *One-two-three-done!* Mary Kate pushed herself out of the pool, shivering on the deck. Her teammate brought her a towel.

"Thanks," she managed and transferred to her wheelchair. She dried off and smiled, feeling warmth in her chest.

We did it.

> *I vividly remember after qualifying for the, for the state meet, you know, being at that state championship, sitting on the blocks, getting ready to swim the first event that athletes with disabilities were gonna have the opportunity to swim in. And, I looked to my left and I looked to my right and I saw eight other female athletes that qualified to be at the state championship. And then I looked around the stadium and I saw all these fans on their feet and cheering on these athletes. And they weren't cheering us on because we were athletes with disabilities, they were cheering us on because we were athletes in that moment.*

***

Mary Kate's case was so inspiring to me during my own case because of how similar the cases were. We had to deal with challenging associations that have existed for decades. Both our cases were dedicated to furthering disability rights in the USA. Challenging the status quo is front and center. I thought if she could do it, then maybe I could too—and, well, here we are.

Mary Kate Callahan (M. Spencer Green/AP/Shutterstock)

Your voice is one of the best tools that you can have in your toolbox, just don't be afraid to use it.

CHAPTER 9
2016

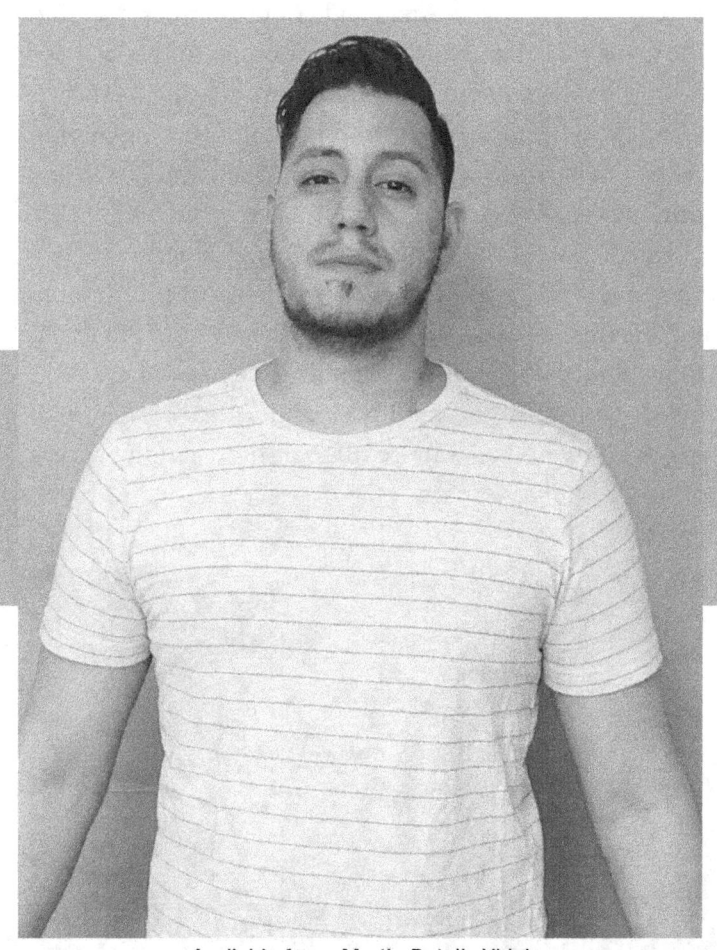

Available from: Martin Batalla Vidal

MARTIN J. BATALLA VIDAL VS. UNJUST DEPORTATION

"I'll see you in court, Mr. President," said Martín (Batalla Vidal, 2019).

The crowd roared. Protesters and counter-protestors alike held signs and chanted their own slogans. In the heart of the protest was Martín J. Batalla Vidal, a rising freshman in college. He stood at a raised podium, wearing a blue T-shirt emblazoned with the words: "Make the Road New York." Make the Road New York was an organization that provided legal services, community organizing, and policy innovation. Their main mission was to assist immigrants and Dreamers—children who were illegally brought to the United States when they were under sixteen and have been raised, educated, and largely consider themselves to be American—who had a more difficult time gaining access to these resources.

Martín speaking at the Home Is Here March: Marching for DACA (Deferred Action for Childhood Arrivals Act) & TPs (Temporary Protected Statuses) (Image provided by Martín J. Batalla Vidal)

Under the presidency of Barack Obama, the Deferred Action for Childhood Arrivals program (DACA) was established. This program gave the Dreamers protection and the ability to legally live in the United States—as well as receive higher level education and employment. However, forty-fifth president Donald J. Trump sought to end this program. This caused distress for many Dreamers because it meant they could potentially be deported to the country they immigrated from, even though many of them hadn't been to those countries since they were too young to remember them.

Fast-forward to 2017. Martín looked out at the crowd at the Home Is Here protest. The protest was taking place just before the first hearing bearing his name: *McAleenan v. Vidal*. He looked over the crowd, which was filled with Dreamers and non-Dreamers alike. Then he caught sight of his mom in the crowd. His eyes welled.

"Don't worry," he said. "We will win." (Batalla Vidal, 2019)

> *DACA is a chance at life, it doesn't define who we are as humans. Whether you have a degree or not, DACA was created for us to come out of the shadows and live freely.*

***

I spoke to Martín, and he had a lot to say about his experience with his Supreme Court case.

> *I still get nervous. Being a plaintiff, people know who you are. I always try to say the right things, but at the end of*

> the day, we're human. I get emotional. That [emotion] is what people love when I do my speeches and rallies. Because, at the end of the day, I'm just a human being that has a heart and is fighting for what I think is right, which is DACA and our right to be in this country.

Although Martín was born in Mexico, he was raised in New York from the age of seven (CitizenPath, 2021). Thus, Martín always considered himself a New Yorker. He went to school in New York, lived in an apartment in New York, and everyone he *knew* lived in New York.

> I knew that I was undocumented, but I grew up like any […] regular American kid. Like, I went to school, I went to the park, I did everything. I went to school, I tried to always have A's in my class, you know, always try to be that good student […] my mother was a single parent. She raised four kids by herself. So, you know, in general, we always try to have good grades to show my mom that her hard work, you know, working two jobs, being a parent, being a father and a mother at the same time, and just telling them that, just so she could see that her- her hard work wasn't in vain.

Despite feeling like a regular New Yorker, Martín still carried many anxieties because of his undocumented status.

✷✷✷

At work, Martín put away his materials and brushed his hands on his scrubs. The gray, overcast sky's vague light flooded in through the windows of the Brain Injury Rehabilitation Center. He looked around for the next brain scan that would be relevant. While walking around the minimalist medical room, he overheard his coworkers talking around the corner.

"Trump got rid of DACA today," one of them said.

Martín sighed, wishing he could go up to his coworkers and tell them just a little of how the loss of DACA would affect him, the person they had worked with for the past year. How he could be deported at any moment. Things *they* had probably never thought about.

> *I always try to be low key about my status [...] So, I tried to do my job and do what I had to do. And I remember the day I was at work, regular day in September [...] we knew that Trump was gonna end DACA from the beginning, that was one of his priorities. And I was just scared 'cause I knew that me losing DACA, I would not be able to work in the medical field.*

Martín had applied for DACA only a few years earlier, two years after he learned of its existence. Because he was undocumented at the time, he was unable to find employment that would enable him to make enough money to pay for an attorney to promote his DACA application in court. Eventually, he found Make the Road New York, a nonprofit that agreed to help Martín through the process. Martín was eventually approved for DACA, and he could live his life in New York without fear. That is, until former President Trump decided to rescind DACA. (Francisco, 2018)

> *[ICE] could come at four in the morning and knock on my door. So that was like, my biggest fear and I felt guilty because, you know, we didn't know what to expect from Trump ending DACA.*

Make the Road New York contacted Martín a few days later. They told him they needed a plaintiff to sue the Trump Administration, and he fit all the criteria.

> *I was gay, I was Mexican, undocumented, I had DACA. So [...] everything worked out perfectly.*

They recruited eight other plaintiffs, and the lawsuit was ready to go. This first lawsuit was dismissed due to lack of evidence, but the Make the Road New York team wasn't ready to give up. They requested and received a second injunction where they were able to make their case.

Martín posing with other plaintiffs in the lawsuit. (Image provided by Martín J. Batalla Vidal)

There were two other lawsuits that took place, *McAleenan v. Vidal* and *Wolf v. Vidal*, all culminating in *New York v. Trump*.

Martín and the Make the Road New York team flooded out of the building and down the Supreme Court stairs. Martín held the Mexican flag to his shoulders like a cape billowing in the wind. Cheers emanated from the crowd and all Martín's anxieties melted away as he walked through the crowd of people chanting, "Home Is Here!" A smile spread across his face, and warmth filled his chest as he made his way to Maryland Avenue, the parade of plaintiffs and allies trailing and jumping behind him. He spotted his mom and hugged her.

"We won, mom," he said as tears streamed down his face. "We won." The SCOTUS decision on DACA was released on June 18, 2020.

Martín posing in front of the Supreme Court building. (Image provided by Martín J. Batalla Vidal)

> ...we would've never thought we had an injunction at a federal level [...] And, we would've never thought that, because of me being crazy, suing the government, it was gonna go to the Supreme Court. And the best feeling that I have is that people all over the country messaged me, "Because of you, I was able to renew DACA twice under President Trump. Thank you so much." And just hearing those words, you inspire me to keep on fighting. When I came out of the Supreme Court, I had the Mexican flag and a lot of people were like, "Oh my god," like, just to see the lead plaintiff coming down the stairs, the highest court, you know, [...] "Fighting for us, for our country, our community, meant so much, inspired me to keep on fighting for immigration reform."

***

When looking at our cases, I can see some differences between them. To start, Martín took on the *president of the United States*. I took on the president of a neighborhood organization. That being said, there are some ways in which our cases are similar. Both of our cases dealt with preserving our rights to live how we wanted in the States, and the consensus is similar as well—we wanted to make the world better, not just for ourselves, but for the kids who would come after us. I became co-chair of the Old Town Triangle Association's accessibility committee, so people of all abilities could live in the Old Town Triangle. Martín became a member of Make the Road New York, and he helps other people eligible for DACA through their process and through obtaining higher education. Martín continued working at the Traumatic Brain Injury Rehabilitation Center after the case.

Martín J. Batalla Vidal (Image provided by Martín J. Batalla Vidal)

I just wanna be a role model. It does not matter where you come from. It does not matter if everybody's against you, just keep on fighting. Honestly, before this whole lawsuit, I had a lot of "no's": "no, no. You're not gonna go nowhere [...] You're just wasting your time." But I knew deep in my heart, you know, like, something was gonna happen. And I went for it, I started speaking, doing rallies, doing one on one, doing a lot of suing, doing a lot of interviews, 'cause I knew eventually this lawsuit was gonna change and it did.

I can't wait to see what he does next.

PART 3

2020s

CHAPTER 10
2021

Available from: Gavin Grimm

GAVIN GRIMM VS. TRANSPHOBIA

Gavin Grimm really had to pee, so he went to the boy's bathroom in his Gloucester, Virginia high school. None of his friends or teachers had a problem with this. After all, we all need to pee. It wasn't until the school board said he had to use the girls' bathroom that Gavin felt humiliated at school. During his freshman year, Gavin had come out as a transgender boy.

> *I used the boys' bathrooms for seven weeks before [...] the first school board meeting happened [...] [The bathrooms] were fine. The important thing about them was that it was the same bathroom all the other boys were using and there were many of them, and so no matter what part of the school campus I was in, there was a bathroom close by.*

He had already legally changed his name to Gavin, begun hormone treatments, and gained special permission from the school principal to use the boys' bathroom when the school board made this call. The board told him he could use private bathrooms, the bathroom in the nurse's office, or the girls' bathroom—but not the boys' bathroom. They began monitoring his bathroom use, forcing him to report back when he had been to the bathroom and where, so they could make sure he was not using the boys' bathroom. As an added side effect to the social humiliation, the bathrooms he was permitted to use were nowhere near his classes, so no matter where he went to pee, he would always be late to class and subsequently capture everyone's attention when he walked into the room.

Gavin continued to advocate for himself, even while his hands shook. He appealed once more to the school board—begging them to regrant him permission to use the boys' bathroom, begging the principal to stop caving and bending to this group of five grown-ups; begging the school board to listen to his peers, the parents of his peers, his teachers—to listen to *him*. However, the board ruled to bar him from the boys' bathrooms—and told him to use unisex or girls' bathrooms. Gavin refused to use either.

> *I didn't go in the girls' rooms. [...] The only bathrooms I would use were the boys' bathroom in the nurses' office.*

Right after that second board meeting, Gavin was angry. "What can I do?" he asked his mom, "How can I fight back?" She could only shake her head in response, speechless.

Gavin's story had already made the news in Virginia, and it was slowly growing in media attention. Families across the nation gathered to see how this would play out. Enter the ACLU.

> *... the ACLU and myself and my mother, who at that time was my legal representative, myself being a minor [met]. [...] It was, "I'm fighting back, I don't care how I do it," and they said, "We'll help you," and I said, "Great, then let's do it."*

Together, the Grimms and the ACLU filed a lawsuit against the Gloucester County school district.

The Grimms lost the first trial in district court, so the Grimms appealed to circuit court. The Fourth US Circuit Court of Appeals, based in Richmond, Virginia, ruled in his favor—it was decided that refusing to let students use bathrooms corresponding to their gender identity would violate the federal law. The ruling cited an Education Department letter from President Barack Obama that stated schools must generally treat transgender students in line with their gender identity—a statement that was considered to be a reasonable interpretation of Title IX (a civil rights law that prohibits discrimination based on sex or gender) at the time. However, when the Trump Administration rescinded the letter in 2016, the Fourth Circuit vacated the ruling. The school pounced on the opportunity and appealed the case to the Supreme Court. The Supreme Court wouldn't hear the case, as it already agreed with the ruling of the lower courts. "A school's policy or actions that treat gay, lesbian, or transgender students differently from other students may cause harm," stated a legal memo from the Department of Education in 2015 (Williams, 2021).

> ...it was fantastic. Incredibly vindicating that the Department of Education itself was like, "Yeah, there's no more wiggle room here, this is the decision, this is what the law says, and these are the policies we expect you to implement." [It is] a cut-and-dried legal matter at this point. They can fight back all they want, and at the end of the day they're going to lose. So that was incredibly vindicating.

Finally, after four years of fighting, Gavin was allowed to use the boys' bathroom—after his high school graduation.

However, despite the unfortunate timing of the ruling, this case marked a turn in the fight for transgender rights in America and provided the reassurance that in time, things will get better.

> *... the only concern I had was whether or not the case was going to continue [...] they could have vacated the case entirely when I graduated and claimed that there was, no reason to continue litigating because I was no longer a student, and so once I knew they were not going to do that, I was like, "Okay, great, sounds good."*

While reflecting on his case, Gavin commented: *"I think one of the most impactful parts of this has been seeing that [...] every passing day there are new students, new children, new young people that are making these changes in their community from the ground up. And even if it seems impossible now, looking at these children, I know, without a doubt, that one day we're gonna have a country, a society that gives them what they deserve, because that's what they believe too."*

In the years since his case, Gavin has had a myriad of achievements. Gavin contributed a chapter to *Nevertheless, We Persisted: 48 Voices of Defiance, Strength, and Courage,* describing his experiences as a transgender man and fighting through his court case. Gavin also wrote the forward for the book *Transgender Students in Elementary School: Creating an Affirming and Inclusive School Culture,* by Melinda M. Mangin. Gavin was also awarded the Courage Award at the Village Voice Pride Awards.

***

Gavin rode in a long, black car down the streets of New York City. A transgender pride flag cape flowed over his shoulders, and he had a teal streak in his hair. He looked over the crowds, each person decked out in rainbows and pride flags, and sung along in his head to the music emanating from the speakers. The audience behind the gates danced along to the music and cheered as Gavin passed by. Under his cape lay a bright rainbow sash with the words "GRAND MARSHAL" printed in large, white lettering. He took a breath and smiled. *This is beautiful.* He fanned himself with his ACLU "RESIST" fan and waved a mini transgender pride flag. Pride swelled in his chest as the car passed more and more landmarks of New York City (Durkee, 2021).

> *I never really felt like anything I was doing was courageous or special because I sorta felt like the circumstances did not leave me a choice in the matter. [...] now, as an adult, when I look back on that fifteen-year-old child, I can acknowledge that it did take courage and bravery to put myself in that position. But at the time, it did not feel remarkable. It felt like I was a victim of circumstance, and accepting accolades for something that I didn't feel I had much agency in was difficult. [...] looking back on it now as an adult who can look at that fifteen-year-old child, with more empathy than I had for myself then, I recognize that it was an incredibly difficult thing to take onto myself. [...] I can understand why the community rallied around me as it did, now, in a way that I didn't necessarily appreciate at the time, thinking, "I don't get all the pomp and circumstance, I'm just some kid, you know, who got discriminated against by the school board. What else is new?"*

***

While looking at Gavin's case, I began to see some similarities and differences between our cases. They were similar in that a vocal, small number of people had been able to shut down Gavin's use of the bathroom, even though they were the only ones complaining. Another similarity was that our cases had to do with typically mundane, everyday places and objects. My case stemmed from my wanting to install a ramp into a garage for days where I needed to use my wheelchair—a need. Gavin's case was stemming from another basic need related to locations that are practically everywhere—bathrooms. However, another similarity between Gavin and myself is that neither of us felt like heroes, and we were largely confused by those who called us brave.

Gavin's story is a prime example of the justice we can all achieve if we work together. Before *Gavin v. Gloucester County,* there had never been a case for transgender rights being heard in the Supreme Court, or past a circuit court in any case. By standing up for himself, Gavin not only put new laws into motion, but also ensured that the next kid wouldn't have to work as hard to be recognized as the gender they identify as. When we stand up for our own rights, often, we stand up for everyone's rights and better the justice system while doing it.

Gavin Grimm (Image provided by Gavin Grimm)

Now, Gavin frequently gives speeches about his experience at schools ranging from preschools and kindergartens to middle schools and high schools. He's noticed, he says, that "those in the younger demographics, looking at their faces and talking to them, they're just getting it."

He continues, "I've realized that these children are our future. They don't have to unlearn gender binary garbage [...] because they're not taking that crap to begin with [...] They're looking to create a future that they think is just, they're looking to create a future that they feel like they deserve. And that is so important to me as an activist and to me as a future educator, a future teacher, to see the children not bogged down by, 'Well, we shouldn't be pushing for this because that's just unobtainable.' They don't know what the hell any of that means. They're not interested in viability politics, they're interested in making a GSA (Gay Students Association) at their elementary school, and they're not asking if they're allowed to do it, they're just doing it."

CHAPTER 11
2021

Available from: Brandi Levy

BRANDI LEVY VS. DIGITAL CENSORSHIP

Brandi had just begun her freshman year at Mahanoy Area High School. She had seen flyers about the tryouts for the varsity cheerleading squad and the softball team, and she was determined to do both.

She mentally rehearsed the cheerleading routine she'd practiced over and over as she lined up for her turn. The line moved slowly, barely inching forward as each hopeful student stepped onto the stage and danced. Brandi's head spun. What if she fell? What if the music didn't play? What if the stage *broke*? The murmur of gossip enveloped her from the front and back of the line. Sharp pain seared through her temples. *Speed up, speed up!*

"Brandi...Levy," the coach enunciated through a megaphone, comfortably slumped in her chair.

Brandi strode onstage, gripping her pompoms in sweaty palms. *One-Two-Three-Four, One-Two-Three-Four,* Brandi chanted under her breath, meticulously measuring out each movement. *One-Two-Three-Four, One-Two-Three-Four— Pose!* Brandi froze, her hands flexed above her head. A sharp breath shot through her ribs as she watched the coach.

"Thank you," the megaphone boomed as the coach wrote a few words on her clipboard. Brandi scuttled off the stage.

> *[The tryouts] were rough. It was for a few days where we practiced and learned everything and then we had our tryouts and we had them with another person. It was us and one other person. And then we'd try out in the gym and we'd go in the locker room. And then after they tallied up everything, we would all go out*

into the gym. We'd have numbers. So they would call out numbers to see who made what team.

Brandi waited excitedly for the announcement. One by one, the friends she had been sitting with were called for varsity. Brandi was crushed when a younger student, an eighth grader, was called for the varsity lineup (de Vogue, 2021).

The rest of the school week went on in the usual routine. Classes droned on with introductions and syllabi, the lunchroom screamed with noise, and the school bells continued to shatter the student body's eardrums. The students who had tried out for softball all awaited the posting with nervous excitement—it was practically all they talked about. Brandi was laughing with her friend in the hall outside her locker, and gathering materials to go home, when she got the softball results on her phone: she wasn't listed.

Brandi was angry for the whole day. After school, she decided she needed to blow off some steam. She and her friend stepped into the parking lot outside the school and Brandi pulled out her phone. They decided on a pose and clicked on the camera. A little emotional relief and then it would be gone forever. Brandi clicked through the filters and emojis and send list, directing it to her social circle. Her friends would *have* to share her sentiment, even the ones who had made the varsity squad! It was unfair, and they would see that. Brandi stuck her tongue out and flipped the middle finger. Her friend's head got cropped out of the photo, but her outfit and middle finger were clearly displayed.

Tap. Tap. They sent out two Snapchats. The captions read: "F*ck school f*ck softball f*ck cheer f*ck everything," and

"Love how me and [another student] get told we need a year of jv before we make varsity but that's doesn't matter to anyone else? 🙄" (de Vogue, 2021; Gersen, 2021) Brandi typed in the captions and pressed "Send." She and her friend then went to hang out at their favorite fast-food place before going home to do their homework. The school week carried on, and nothing really changed except for the seeming weight of the world falling off Brandi's shoulders. A few affirming comments appeared under Brandi's Snapchat, encouraging her to keep pushing forward. For the first time since the posting, Brandi felt that everything just might be okay.

∗∗∗

Brandi was in homeroom as usual. The teacher droned on as students' eyes scoured the clock, wishing the red hand would move just a little faster. Brandi was seated in the middle row of the classroom, just the way she liked it. Not so close that you would get teacher spittle on your face, but not too far away that you had to squint to see what they were writing on the board.

A sharp beep emitted from the teacher's phone. The teacher picked up the phone, listened for a moment, and turned to Brandi.

"Brandi, the cheer coach wants to see you in her classroom."

Brandi looked around, suddenly tense. All eyes were on her as she packed up her bag and pencils. The teacher drew out the hallway pass and handed it to her with a quizzical look.

Brandi walked down the hallway, her mind racing. *What could I have done?* She had never been called to a coach's classroom before. Something must have happened. *Maybe the school bus has been canceled?* No, that didn't make sense. Her knees bowed as she neared the classroom. Every squeaky sneaker step weighed exponentially heavier as she neared her destination.

There was no one in there [the office] when I went.

Brandi inched into the classroom, squirming as she searched for signs of life. *Maybe there had been a mistake...*

"Ah, Brandi Levy," a voice rang out from an office just off the classroom. "Please come in."

Brandi hesitated before moving in the direction of the office door.

"Sit, sit," the coach told her.

"Is everything alright?" Brandi looked around, noting that the classroom was empty.

"No."

Brandi blinked quickly. "Why? What did I do?"

"Does this look familiar?" The coach showed Brandi a screenshot.

Brandi's eyes widened and she gasped. *My Snapchat.* But how? She had only sent it to her friends. She stiffened. *The cheerleaders.* Some of her friends were on the cheerleading squad. It had to have been them. Brandi squeezed her eyes shut and buried her head in her hands, ready to hear her sentence.

The school board decided on a year-long suspension from the cheer team. She violated school policy, they said. They told her that she had used "inappropriate" and "upsetting" language.

They told me that I'm lucky I didn't get expelled from school for it because it was vulgar language. (CNN, 2021)

Brandi's mind went blank. She had never heard of the school giving out a team suspension without a warning. She began to doubt herself. Maybe she *had* really had this much of a negative effect on her peers. But people cursed and vented on Snapchat all the time—was what she had sent really *that* bad? Confusion filled her head. *I guess it must have been that bad.*

As time went on, however, it seemed like Brandi's words hadn't really affected anyone. Classes continued as normal, and there were no further reports of students being distressed by Brandi's Snapchat post. Brandi's father, Larry Levy, appealed to the school board—saying it was a parental issue for a child to be disciplined, not the school. He went to the board meetings, asking them to give Brandi a different punishment. They refused.

Finally, Larry and Brandi had had enough and filed a lawsuit against the entire Mahanoy Area School District, claiming Brandi's right to freedom of speech had been violated. Their argument was that Brandi's Snapchat had been off-campus and had contained nothing that alluded to her school. The words she had used were generic: "f*ck school" and "*f*ck cheer," and she had not been wearing any clothing with the school logo.

> *I'm pretty sure I remember [the rules in the Code of Conduct] in the rules, it did not have anything about what I can and can't say out of school, and out of my uniform.* (CNN, 2021)

The case grew into a federal lawsuit. The argument stated the school had clearly violated her First Amendment rights, and the year-long team suspension assigned to her was unconstitutional. Eventually, the federal court ruled in Brandi's favor. Upon hearing of the ruling, the school appealed the case to the state Supreme Court, where Brandi would fight for the next three years. With the help of the American Civil Liberties Union (ACLU) and attorney Sara Rose, Brandi was able to fight the Mahanoy Area School District's ruling (Oyez, 2022).

On June 23, 2021, Brandi finally received the ruling from the Supreme Court justices. It was eight to one—in her favor.

"The fact that Petitioner claims it can punish B.L. for a momentary expression of frustration on a weekend out of school and out of season shows how sweeping its approach is. Its rule would teach students they can never speak candidly with their friends without worrying that a school official will deem their views potentially disruptive and suspend them or otherwise punish them. That is exactly the wrong lesson to teach. Thank you."
—ACLU National Legal Director David D. Cole (Oyez, 2021).

Brandi's case was key in the discussion surrounding free speech, its effect on school, and how technology affects both. The main question being, when should the school (and by extension, the government) get involved in the online lives of students? And, should students' speech outside school be as regulated as it is when they are inside school walls? In Brandi's case, her Snaps were not targeted at anyone within the school. They were general statements that contained no names, no school affiliation, and were off campus. Because of these factors, if it had not been online, the comments would likely have been dismissed and Brandi would not have faced a year-long suspension. In cases like *Tinker v. Des Moines*, the subject of freedom of speech at school has been front and center, but off-campus speech had yet to make an appearance on the courtroom floor. With Brandi's win, students could now safely say that free speech outside of school is not regulated by the government.

Brandi Levy (Image provided by Brandi Levy)

I mean, [the] winning the Supreme Court part was what stuck with me. Especially coming from a small town in a small community, it was really a game changer for everybody here [in Pennsylvania] [...] it's going to control a lot more of how students get punished.

CONCLUSION

I learned so much from interviewing the teen heroes featured in this book and hearing about their activism firsthand. All of their stories were so different, but they had two common threads. First, the world can be full of really hard challenges—difficult situations, people who treat others badly. Second, no matter how bleak things seem, people still gravitate toward hope and compassion for themselves and others. The stories in this book highlight our common need for connection, understanding, and hope for a better, brighter future together.

Hope motivated me to reach out to the other activists in this book. I reached out to learn more about who they were as people. Through these conversations, I felt less alone in my fight for disability rights and even more motivated to fight for change.

A lot of work still needs to be done in terms of civil rights and liberties, and it's up to us.

Sometimes activism will choose you—as it chose me and others in this book. Other times, you will get to choose what you will support, which injustice you will face down, who you will speak for, and how you will engage. If we all work together, we can achieve a better world.

No matter how you become an activist, one thing is for certain: if we work together, we can make tomorrow begin now.

ACKNOWLEDGMENTS

Hi! If you made it to the end of this book, I am thoroughly impressed. Thank you so much for dedicating some of your time to reading this book. It really means the world to me.

Thank you to everyone who helped make this book possible—including readers like you!

Thank you to my attorneys for helping me get resources to help write about my own case, helping me secure some of the interviews in this book, and for endlessly supporting me during the lawsuit: Nick Ftikas, Mary Rosenberg, Ken Walden, Michael Allen, Perry Abdulkadir, and Tahir Duckett. You all made this journey, through the lawsuit and writing this book, far more manageable; you all did an amazing job of reassuring me during the lawsuit, no matter how scared I was. Thank you.

Thank you to the lawyers, journalists, and authors I cold-emailed who helped me get in contact with a few of these activists. I am honestly still stunned that you all actually responded. Thank you.

Thank you to my editors Shanna Heath and John Chancey for making this book the best it could be and helping me sort out how to write all these stories.

Thank you to everyone I interviewed for taking time out of your day to help me out: Aaron Fricke, Angel Rodriguez, Brandi Levy, Bridgetta Bourne-Firl, Constance McMillen, Gavin Grimm, Heidi Rodriguez, Martín Batalla Vidal, Mary Beth Tinker, Mary Kate Callahan, Minnijean Brown Trickey, Najah Najiy, and Silissa Uriarte-Smith.

Thank you to everyone who pre-ordered and donated to my book. You all were essential to bringing this book to life. As promised, all of you are listed here:

Aimee Wertepny, Alex Fogel, Alp Demirtas, Amanda Carr, Andrew Diehlmann, Anna Bohlen, Annabelle Deakin, Annie Schaffer, apollonia666, Ariadne Merchant, Asher Grossman, Ava Wilczak, Ben Stankiewicz, Benjamin Myers, Benjamin Sachs, Bill Deakin, Camille Baughn-Cunningham, Chloe Deakin, Chloe Ma, Christine Sullivan, Conor Daly, Darren Fuller, David Galindo, Destiny Strange, Donna Shamis, Elvi Casia, Eric Koester, Erica Cheung, Erica Swarts, Francisco Javier Saez de Adana, Giselle Escobedo, Henry Deakin, Inga Domenick, Jane Barnard, Jason Altmann, Jay Deakin, Jayne Crouthamel, Jean Deakin, Jennifer Tam, Jessica Farley, Joey Zisk, Judy Murray, Kara Tao, Karen Lurie, Kathleen O'Connor, Kathy Orndoff, Khairy Shakir Barnes, Kian Quinn, Kriti Sarav, Lan Zhang, Laura W. Doto, Laura Wigger, Lauren Kilpatrick, Lauren Tapper, Lisa Diehlmann, Lucy Biederman, Lucy Nathwani, Malerie Williams, Mandy Bunte, Mary Hadley, Matthew Landa, Maya El Shamsy, Michael Allen, Michael

Wong, Midge May, Mythili Venkataraman, Nicholas Wayne Pietraszek, Nick Emerton, Nicole Neal, Perry Abdulkadir, Phoebe Myers, Rebecca Wigger, Ryan Allen, Ryan Hudec, Sara Christine Chojnacki, Sarah A. Kalmenson Pinson, Sarah Tetedje, Satish Shenoy, Selom Tetedje, Sharyq Siddiqi, Shirley DeLong, Stephanie Diehlmann, Sterling Kennedy, Susan Augustine, tetra was here, Thaddeus Andracki, W. Danielle Jones, William Hoffman, and Yannik Leuz.

Finally, I want to thank Ms. Storm, my eighth-grade humanities teacher. Your class was where I first read *Warriors Don't Cry*, and it was also you who was so supportive of me during the lawsuit. You encouraged me to continue reaching out to civil rights activists and made sure to regularly check in on me. You also helped build my confidence in history classes with your fun, musical way of teaching—a subject I was not totally confident in before your class—and your enthusiasm that I was met with every time we talked about anything, really. Thank you.

APPENDIX

PREFACE

Access Living. "Who We Are." Accessed February 16, 2022.
https://www.accessliving.org/who-we-are/.

ACLU. "Tinker v. Des Moines - Landmark Supreme Court Ruling on Behalf of Student Expression." Accessed February 16, 2022.
https://www.aclu.org/other/tinker-v-des-moines-landmark-supreme-court-ruling-behalf-student-expression.

Cornell Law School. "Appeal." Accessed June 30, 2022.
https://www.law.cornell.edu/wex/appeal.

Cornell Law School. "Lawsuit." Accessed June 30, 2022.
https://www.law.cornell.edu/wex/lawsuit.

Cornell Law School. "Plaintiff." Accessed June 30, 2022.
https://www.law.cornell.edu/wex/plaintiff.

Cornell Law School. "Protected Class." Accessed June 30, 2022.
https://www.law.cornell.edu/wex/protected_class.

Cornell Law School. "Protest." Accessed June 30, 2022.
https://www.law.cornell.edu/wex/protest.

Cornell Law School. "Represent." Accessed June 30, 2022.
https://www.law.cornell.edu/wex/represent.

Dover, Lynn. "What Is a 'Protected Class?'" Law Offices of Kimball Tirey & St. John LLP. Last updated January, 2020.
https://www.kts-law.com/what-is-a-protected-class/.

McLaughlin, Carter. "What Makes a Chosen One: A Trope Analysis." *West Side Story,* May 2, 2021.
https://wsspaper.com/68256/ae/what-makes-a-chosen-one-a-trope-analysis/.

United States Courts. "About the US Courts of Appeals." Accessed June 30, 2022. https://www.uscourts.gov/about-federal-courts/court-role-and-structure/about-us-courts-appeals.

United States Department of Justice. "Introduction to the Federal Court System." Accessed February 22, 2022. https://www.justice.gov/usao/justice-101/federal-courts.

CHAPTER 1: AVA DEAKIN V. ABLEISM IN HISTORIC DISTRICTS (2019)

Access Living of Metropolitan Chicago. "Written Statement in Support of 1848 N. Lincoln Avenue." November 16, 2018.

Ballew, Jonathan. "Historic Old Town Building Would Look 'Horrible' with Accessible Garage for Teen in Wheelchair, Neighbors Say." Block Club Chicago, November 15, 2018. https://blockclubchicago.org/2018/11/15/historic-old-town-building-would-look-horrible-with-accessible-garage-for-teen-in-wheelchair-neighbors-say/.

Harris, Jasmine E. "The Aesthetics of Disability." *Columbia Law Review* 119, no.4 (May 2019): 949. https://columbialawreview.org/content/the-aesthetics-of-disability.

Murphy, Shelly, Sasha Mayoras, Vi Daley, and Philip Graff. "Urgent! OTTA Election January '21 - Important Considerations." NextDoor. Last modified January 7, 2021. https://nextdoor.com/p/f-cW3ypqzHLZ?view=detail.

Old Town Triangle Association. "Historic District / Planning & Zoning Committee." Accessed March 2, 2022. https://www.oldtowntriangle.com/about/committees/historic-district-planning-zoning-2/.

CHAPTER 2: MINNIJEAN BROWN TRICKEY V. SEGREGATION (1957)

Bennett, Brad. "Little Rock Nine: Decades-Long Battle for School Equity Began with Nine Black Students Facing Angry White Mob." Southern Poverty Law Center. September 25, 2020. https://www.splcenter.org/news/2020/09/25/little-rock-nine-decades-long-battle-school-equity-began-nine-black-students-facing-angry.

Duignan, Brian. "Plessy v. Ferguson." *Encyclopedia Britannica*, May 11, 2022. https://www.britannica.com/event/Plessy-v-Ferguson-1896.

History. "Brown v. Board of Education." Last updated January 11, 2022. https://www.history.com/topics/black-history/brown-v-board-of-education-of-topeka.

Lavin. "Minnijean Brown Trickey." Accessed June 28, 2022. https://www.thelavinagency.com/speakers/minnijean-brown-trickey.

Little Rock Culture Vulture. "Little Rock Look Back: Minnijean Brown Trickey."
September 11, 2017.
https://lrculturevulture.com/2017/09/11/little-rock-look-back-minnijean-brown-trickey/.

Little Rock Nine Foundation. "Little Rock Nine Members." Accessed June 28, 2022.
https://www.littlerock9.com/members.html.

Millard Fillmore's Bathtub. "Little Rock's Central High School, Monument for Civil Rights." Accessed June 28, 2022.
https://timpanogos.blog/2011/07/01/little-rocks-central-high-school-monument-for-civil-rights/.

Pattillo-Beals, Melba. *Warriors Don't Cry: A Searing Memoir of the Battle to Integrate Little Rock's Central High.* Washington Square Press, 1994.

Smithsonian's History Explorer. "Minnijean Brown-Trickey's Suspension Notice February 6, 1958." December 30, 2020.
https://historyexplorer.si.edu/resource/minnijean-brown-trickeys-suspension-notice-february-6-1958.

The Editors of Encyclopedia Britannica. "Spingarn Medal." *Encyclopedia Britannica*, April 25, 2021.
https://www.britannica.com/topic/Spingarn-Medal.

Thirteen: Media with Impact. "Minnijean Brown Trickey, Environmental and Civil Rights Activist." March 26, 2009.
https://www.thirteen.org/unsungheroines/women-cat/minnijean-brown-trickey-environmental-and-civil-rights-activist/.

CHAPTER 3: NAJAH NAJIY V. RACIAL INEQUALITY (1963)

Clark, Alexis. "The Children's Crusade: When the Youth of Birmingham Marched for Justice." History. Last updated January 28, 2021.
https://www.history.com/news/childrens-crusade-birmingham-civil-rights.

History.com Editors. "Civil Rights Act of 1964." History. Last updated January 20, 2022.
https://www.history.com/topics/black-history/civil-rights-act.

King, Martin Luther. "The Negro Is Your Brother." *The Atlantic Monthly* 212, no. 2 (August 1963): 78–88.
https://www.csuchico.edu/iege/_assets/documents/susi-letter-from-birmingham-jail.pdf.

CHAPTER 4: MARY BETH TINKER V. CENSORSHIP (1969)

ACLU. "Tinker v. Des Moines - Landmark Supreme Court Ruling on Behalf of Student Expression." Accessed March 14, 2022.
https://www.aclu.org/other/tinker-v-des-moines-landmark-supreme-court-ruling-behalf-student-expression.

ACLU Iowa. "Mary Beth Tinker Reflects on Being a Student Rights Pioneer." Accessed June 26, 2022.
https://www.aclu-ia.org/en/mary-beth-tinker-reflects-being-student-rights-pioneer.

National Archives. "Vietnam War US Military Fatal Casualty Statistics." Last modified April 29, 2008.
https://www.archives.gov/research/military/vietnam-war/casualty-statistics.

The Editors of Encyclopedia Britannica. "How Many People Died in the Vietnam War?" *Encyclopedia Britannica*, April 28, 2020.
https://www.britannica.com/question/How-many-people-died-in-the-Vietnam-War.

Tinker Tour. "Mary Beth Tinker." Accessed March 14, 2022.
https://tinkertourusa.org/about/tinkerbio/.

CHAPTER 5: AARON FRICKE V. HOMOPHOBIA (1980)
Fricke v. Lynch, 491 F. Supp. 381 (D.R.I. 1980).
https://law.justia.com/cases/federal/district-courts/FSupp/491/381/1799237/.

CHAPTER 6: BRIDGETTA BOURNE-FIRL V. ABLEISM AGAINST DEAF PEOPLE (1988)
California State University. "Biography: Yoon Lee." April, 2005.
http://www.csun.edu/deaffilms2005/bio.html#lee.

DPN Undocumented Voices of Women Leaders. "Deaf President Now (DPN) Movement of 1988: Undocumented Voices of Deaf Women Leaders- BB Bourne-Firl." August 13, 2019. Video, 48:16.
https://www.youtube.com/watch?v=X1Aayyn-J1Q.

Lee, Yoon. "In Their Own Words: Yoon Lee." *Gallaudet University,* accessed June 3, 2022.
https://www.gallaudet.edu/about/history-and-traditions/deaf-president-now/profiles-and-viewpoints/in-their-own-words/.

CHAPTER 7: CONSTANCE MCMILLEN V. HOMOPHOBIA (2010)
ACLU. "ACLU Complaint Takes on 'Decoy' Prom for Mississippi Lesbian Student." April 21, 2010.
https://www.aclu.org/press-releases/aclu-complaint-takes-decoy-prom-mississippi-lesbian-student.

ACLU of San Diego & Imperial Counties. "Constance McMillen's Prom Story." July 16, 2010. Video, 4:00.
https://www.youtube.com/watch?v=q4aNnfqMoKU.

Clips 6. "Constance McMillen CBS Interview." March 12, 2010. Video, 3:34.
https://www.youtube.com/watch?v=huvL3SoThPo.

GLAAD. "Constance McMillen at the 21st Annual GLAAD Media Awards in Los Angeles." April 20, 2010. Video, 2:28.
https://www.youtube.com/watch?v=8hKvktQDGQI.

McMillen v. Itawamba County School District, 702 F. Supp. 2d 699 (N.D. Miss. 2010).

On Top Magazine Staff. "Gay Teen Denied Prom Constance McMillen Story Coming to ABC Family." *On Top Magazine,* October 9, 2010.
http://www.ontopmag.com/article/6559/Gay_Teen_Denied_Prom_Constance_McMillen_Story_Coming_To_ABC_Family.

Perez Hilton (blog). "Constance Is Coming to Hollywood!" March 16, 2010.
https://perezhilton.com/constance-is-coming-to-hollywood/.

TheEllenShow. "Constance McMillen Talks about Her Fight for Equality." October 12, 2010. Video, 7:22.
https://www.youtube.com/watch?v=B9bZcOsdWt8.

CHAPTER 8: MARY KATE CALLAHAN V. ABLEISM IN SPORTS (2012)

Equip for Equality. "Madigan and Callahan v. Illinois High School Association, 12-cv-3758 (N.D. Illinois May 16, 2012)." Last updated May 11, 2018.
https://www.equipforequality.org/news-item/callahan/.

National Women's History Museum. "Mary Kate Callahan." Accessed June 1, 2022.
https://www.womenshistory.org/mary-kate-callahan.

Sports Litigation Alert. "Federal Court Sides with Disabled Athlete in Suit against Illinois High School Association." October 19, 2012.
https://sportslitigationalert.com/federal-court-sides-with-disabled-athlete-in-suit-against-illinois-high-school-association/.

CHAPTER 9: MARTÍN J. BATALLA VIDAL V. UNJUST DEPORTATION (2016)

Batalla Vidal, Martín. "The Supreme Court Will Hear My Case Today. Trump Will Not Win on DACA." *Vox,* November 12, 2019.
https://www.vox.com/first-person/2019/11/12/20953221/daca-supreme-court-immigrants.

CitizenPath. "DACA Benefits – Three Dreamer Success Stories." June 15, 2021.
https://citizenpath.com/daca-benefits-success-stories/.

Francisco, Noel J. "Kirstjen M. Nielsen, Secretary of Homeland Security, et al., Petitioners v. Martin Jonathan Batalla Vidal, et al." Legal document, Washington, DC, 2018.
https://www.supremecourt.gov/DocketPDF/18/18-589/71034/20181105135257794_Nielsen%20v.%20Batalla%20Vidal%20-%20App.pdf.

CHAPTER 10: GAVIN GRIMM V. TRANSPHOBIA (2021)

Durkee, Alison. "Supreme Court Declines to Hear Landmark Transgender Bathroom Case, Leaving Gavin Grimm Victory in Place." *Forbes*, last updated June 28, 2021. https://www.forbes.com/sites/alisondurkee/2021/06/28/supreme-court-declines-to-hear-landmark-transgender-bathroom-case-leaving-gavin-grimm-victory-in-place/?sh=5c6ce3a57176.

Williams, Pete. "Supreme Court Won't Hear Dispute over Bathrooms for Transgender Students." *NBC*, last modified June 28, 2021. https://www.nbcnews.com/politics/supreme-court/supreme-court-won-t-hear-dispute-over-bathrooms-transgender-students-n1272513.

CHAPTER 11: BRANDI LEVY V. DIGITAL CENSORSHIP (2021)

CNN. "High School Cheerleader Suspended for Explicit Snapchat Speaks Out." January 2, 2021. Video, 8:57. https://www.youtube.com/watch?v=y5jTc-3Jj8I.

de Vogue, Ariane. "Supreme Court Grapples with First Amendment Rights of Schoolchildren in Cheerleader Case." *CNN*, last updated April 28, 2021. https://www.cnn.com/2021/04/28/politics/supreme-court-first-amendment-cheerleader-brandi-levy/index.html.

Gersen, Jeannie Suk. "The Complicated Case of the Pennsylvania Cheerleader." *The New Yorker*, May 6, 2021. https://www.newyorker.com/news/our-columnists/the-complicated-case-of-the-pennsylvania-cheerleader.

Oyez. "Mahanoy Area School District v. B.L." Accessed June 21, 2022. https://www.oyez.org/cases/2020/20-255.

www.ingramcontent.com/pod-product-compliance
Lightning Source LLC
LaVergne TN
LVHW012021060526
838201LV00061B/4394